THE ART OF WAR

THE OLDEST MILITARY TREATISE IN THE WORLD

by SUN TZU

Translated by Lionel Giles

A BOOK OF FIVE RINGS

by Miyamoto Musashi

Translated by D.W.

THE ART OF WAR
THE OLDEST MILITARY TREATISE IN THE WORLD

by SUN TZU

Translated from the Chinese
By LIONEL GILES.

THE ART OF WAR

CHAPTER I: LAYING PLANS

1. Sun Tzu said: The art of war is of vital importance to the State.

2. It is a matter of life and death, a road either to safety or to ruin. Hence it is a subject of inquiry which can on no account be neglected.

3. The art of war, then, is governed by five constant factors, to be taken into account in one's deliberations when seeking to determine the conditions obtaining in the field.

4. These are: (1) The Moral Law; (2) Heaven; (3) Earth; (4) The Commander; (5) Method and discipline.

5, 6. The Moral Law causes the people to be in complete accord with their ruler, so that they will follow him regardless of their lives, undismayed by any danger.

7. Heaven signifies night and day, cold and heat, times and seasons.

8. Earth comprises distances great and small; danger and security; open ground and narrow passes; the chances of life and death.

9. The Commander stands for the virtues of wisdom,

sincerety, benevolence, courage and strictness.

10. By method and discipline are to be understood the marshalling of the army in its proper subdivisions, the graduations of rank among the officers, the maintenance of roads by which supplies may reach the army, and the control of military expenditure.

11. These five heads should be familiar to every general. He who knows them will be victorious; he who knows them not will fail.

12. Therefore, in your deliberations, when seeking to determine the military conditions, let them be made the basis of a comparison, in this wise:

13. (1) Which of the two sovereigns is imbued with the Moral law?
(2) Which of the two generals has the most ability?
(3) With whom lie the advantages derived from Heaven and Earth?
(4) On which side is discipline most rigorously enforced?
(5) Which army is stronger?
(6) On which side are officers and men more highly trained?
(7) In which army is there the greater constancy both in reward and punishment?

14. By means of these seven considerations I can forecast victory or defeat.

15. The general that hearkens to my counsel and acts upon

it will conquer. Let such a one be retained in command! The general that hearkens not to my counsel nor acts upon it, will suffer defeat. Let such a one be dismissed!

16. While heeding the profit of my counsel, avail yourself also of any helpful circumstances over and beyond the ordinary rules.

17. According as circumstances are favorable, one should modify one's plans.

18. All warfare is based on deception.

19. Hence, when able to attack, we must seem unable; when using our forces, we must seem inactive; when we are near, we must make the enemy believe we are far away; when far away, we must make him believe we are near.

20. Hold out baits to entice the enemy. Feign disorder and crush him.

21. If he is secure at all points, be prepared for him. If he is in superior strength, evade him.

22. If your opponent is of choleric temper, seek to irritate him. Pretend to be weak that he may grow arrogant.

23. If he is taking his ease, give him no rest. If his forces are united, separate them.

24. Attack him where he is unprepared; appear where you

are not expected.

25. These military devices, leading to victory, must not be divulged beforehand.

26. Now the general who wins a battle makes many calculations in his temple ere the battle is fought. The general who loses a battle makes but few calculations beforehand. Thus do many calculations lead to victory, and few calculations to defeat. How much more so no calculation at all! It is by attention to this point that I can foresee who is likely to win or lose.

CHAPTER II: WAGING WAR

1. Sun Tzu said: In the operations of war, where there are in the field a thousand swift chariots, as many heavy chariots, and a hundred thousand mail-clad soldiers, with provisions enough to carry them a thousand li, then the expenditure at home and at the front -- including entertainment of guests, small items such as glue and paint, and sums spent on chariots and armor -- will reach the total of a thousand ounces of silver per day. Such is the cost of raising an army of 100,000 men.

2. When you engage in actual fighting, if victory is long in coming, then men's weapons will grow dull and their ardor will be damped. If you lay siege to a town, you will exhaust your strength.

3. Again, if the campaign is protracted, the resources of the State will not be equal to the strain.

4. Now, when your weapons are dulled, your ardor damped, your strength exhausted and your treasure spent, other chieftains will spring up to take advantage of your extremity. Then no man, however wise, will be able to avert the consequences that must ensue.

5. Thus, though we have heard of stupid haste in war, cleverness has never been seen associated with long delays.

6. There is no instance of a country having benefited from prolonged warfare.

7. It is only one who is thoroughly acquainted with the evils of war that can thoroughly understand the profitable way of carrying it on.

8. The skillful soldier does not raise a second levy, neither are his supply-wagons loaded more than twice.

9. Bring war material with you from home, but forage on the enemy. Thus the army will have food enough for its needs.

10. Poverty of the State exchequer causes an army to be maintained by contributions from a distance. Contributing to maintain an army at a distance causes the people to be impoverished.

11. On the other hand, the proximity of an army causes prices to go up, and high prices cause the people's substance to be drained away.

12. When their substance is drained away, the peasantry will be afflicted by heavy exactions.

13,14. With this loss of substance and exhaustion of strength, the homes of the people will be stripped bare, and three-tenths of their income will be dissipated, while government expenses for broken chariots, worn-out horses, breast-plates and helmets, bows and arrows, spears and shields, protective mantles, draught-oxen and heavy wagons, will amount to four-tenths of its total revenue.

15. Hence a wise general makes a point of foraging on the enemy. One cartload of the enemy's provisions is equivalent to twenty of one's own, and likewise a single picul of his provender is equivalent to twenty from one's own store.

16. Now in order to kill the enemy, our men must be roused to anger; that there may be advantage from defeating the enemy, they must have their rewards.

17. Therefore in chariot fighting, when ten or more chariots have been taken, those should be rewarded who took the first. Our own flags should be substituted for those of the enemy, and the chariots mingled and used in conjunction with ours. The captured soldiers should be kindly treated and kept.

18. This is called using the conquered foe to augment one's own strength.

19. In war, then, let your great object be victory, not lengthy campaigns.

20. Thus it may be known that the leader of armies is the arbiter of the people's fate, the man on whom it depends whether the nation shall be in peace or in peril.

THE ART OF WAR

CHAPTER III: ATTACK BY STRATAGEM

1. Sun Tzu said: In the practical art of war, the best thing of all is to take the enemy's country whole and intact; to shatter and destroy it is not so good. So, too, it is better to capture an army entire than to destroy it, to capture a regiment, a detachment or a company entire than to destroy them.

2. Hence to fight and conquer in all your battles is not supreme excellence; supreme excellence consists in breaking the enemy's resistance without fighting.

3. Thus the highest form of generalship is to balk the enemy's plans; the next best is to prevent the junction of the enemy's forces; the next in order is to attack the enemy's army in the field; and the worst policy of all is to besiege walled cities.

4. The rule is not to besiege walled cities if it can possibly be avoided. The preparation of mantlets, movable shelters, and various implements of war, will take up three whole months, and the piling up of mounds over against the walls will take three months more.

5. The general, unable to control his irritation, will launch his men to the assault like swarming ants, with the result that one-third of his men are slain, while the town still

remains untaken. Such are the disastrous effects of a siege.

6. Therefore, the skillful leader subdues the enemy's troops without any fighting; he captures their cities without laying siege to them; he overthrows their kingdom without lengthy operations in the field.

7. With his forces intact he will dispute the mastery of the Empire, and thus, without losing a man, his triumph will be complete. This is the method of attacking by stratagem.

8. It is the rule in war, if our forces are ten to the enemy's one, to surround him; if five to one, to attack him; if twice as numerous, to divide our army into two.

9. If equally matched, we can offer battle; if slightly inferior in numbers, we can avoid the enemy; if quite unequal in every way, we can flee from him.

10. Hence, though an obstinate fight may be made by a small force, in the end it must be captured by the larger force.

11. Now the general is the bulwark of the State. If the bulwark is complete at all points, the State will be strong; if the bulwark is defective, the State will be weak.

12. There are three ways in which a ruler can bring misfortune upon his army:

13. (1) By commanding the army to advance or to retreat, being ignorant of the fact that it cannot obey. This is called

hobbling the army.

14. (2) By attempting to govern an army in the same way as he administers a kingdom, being ignorant of the conditions which obtain in an army. This causes restlessness in the soldiers' minds.

15. (3) By employing the officers of his army without discrimination, through ignorance of the military principle of adaptation to circumstances. This shakes the confidence of the soldiers.

16. But when the army is restless and distrustful, trouble is sure to come from the other feudal princes. This is simply bringing anarchy into the army, and flinging victory away.

17. Thus we may know that there are five essentials for victory:

(1) He will win who knows when to fight and when not to fight.
(2) He will win who knows how to handle both superior and inferior forces.
(3) He will win whose army is animated by the same spirit throughout all its ranks.
(4) He will win who, prepared himself, waits to take the enemy unprepared.
(5) He will win who has military capacity and is not interfered with by the sovereign.

18. Hence the saying: If you know the enemy and know

yourself, you need not fear the result of a hundred battles. If you know yourself but not the enemy, for every victory gained you will also suffer a defeat. If you know neither the enemy nor yourself, you will succumb in every battle.

CHAPTER IV: TACTICAL DISPOSITIONS

1. Sun Tzu said: The good fighters of old first put themselves beyond the possibility of defeat, and then waited for an opportunity of defeating the enemy.

2. To secure ourselves against defeat lies in our own hands, but the opportunity of defeating the enemy is provided by the enemy himself.

3. Thus the good fighter is able to secure himself against defeat, but cannot make certain of defeating the enemy.

4. Hence the saying: One may know how to conquer without being able to do it.

5. Security against defeat implies defensive tactics; ability to defeat the enemy means taking the offensive.

6. Standing on the defensive indicates insufficient strength; attacking, a superabundance of strength.

7. The general who is skilled in defense hides in the most secret recesses of the earth; he who is skilled in attack flashes forth from the topmost heights of heaven. Thus on the one hand we have ability to protect ourselves; on the other, a victory that is complete.

8. To see victory only when it is within the ken of the common herd is not the acme of excellence.

9. Neither is it the acme of excellence if you fight and conquer and the whole Empire says, "Well done!"

10. To lift an autumn hair is no sign of great strength; to see the sun and moon is no sign of sharp sight; to hear the noise of thunder is no sign of a quick ear.

11. What the ancients called a clever fighter is one who not only wins, but excels in winning with ease.

12. Hence his victories bring him neither reputation for wisdom nor credit for courage.

13. He wins his battles by making no mistakes. Making no mistakes is what establishes the certainty of victory, for it means conquering an enemy that is already defeated.

14. Hence the skillful fighter puts himself into a position which makes defeat impossible, and does not miss the moment for defeating the enemy.

15. Thus it is that in war the victorious strategist only seeks battle after the victory has been won, whereas he who is destined to defeat first fights and afterwards looks for victory.

16. The consummate leader cultivates the moral law, and strictly adheres to method and discipline; thus it is in his power to control success.

17. In respect of military method, we have, firstly, Measurement; secondly, Estimation of quantity; thirdly, Calculation; fourthly, Balancing of chances; fifthly, Victory.

18. Measurement owes its existence to Earth; Estimation of quantity to Measurement; Calculation to Estimation of quantity; Balancing of chances to Calculation; and Victory to Balancing of chances.

19. A victorious army opposed to a routed one, is as a pound's weight placed in the scale against a single grain.

20. The onrush of a conquering force is like the bursting of pent-up waters into a chasm a thousand fathoms deep.

THE ART OF WAR

CHAPTER V: ENERGY

1. Sun Tzu said: The control of a large force is the same principle as the control of a few men: it is merely a question of dividing up their numbers.

2. Fighting with a large army under your command is nowise different from fighting with a small one: it is merely a question of instituting signs and signals.

3. To ensure that your whole host may withstand the brunt of the enemy's attack and remain unshaken -- this is effected by maneuvers direct and indirect.

4. That the impact of your army may be like a grindstone dashed against an egg -- this is effected by the science of weak points and strong.

5. In all fighting, the direct method may be used for joining battle, but indirect methods will be needed in order to secure victory.

6. Indirect tactics, efficiently applied, are inexhaustible as Heaven and Earth, unending as the flow of rivers and streams. Like the sun and moon, they end but to begin anew; like the four seasons, they pass away to return once more.

7. There are not more than five musical notes, yet the combinations of these five give rise to more melodies than

can ever be heard.

8. There are not more than five primary colors (blue, yellow, red, white, and black), yet in combination they produce more hues than can ever been seen.

9. There are not more than five cardinal tastes (sour, acrid, salt, sweet, bitter), yet combinations of them yield more flavors than can ever be tasted.

10. In battle, there are not more than two methods of attack -- the direct and the indirect, yet these two in combination give rise to an endless series of maneuvers.

11. The direct and the indirect lead on to each other in turn. It is like moving in a circle -- you never come to an end. Who can exhaust the possibilities of their combination?

12. The onset of troops is like the rush of a torrent which will even roll stones along in its course.

13. The quality of decision is like the well-timed swoop of a falcon which enables it to strike and destroy its victim.

14. Therefore the good fighter will be terrible in his onset, and prompt in his decision.

15. Energy may be likened to the bending of a crossbow; decision, to the releasing of a trigger.

16. Amid the turmoil and tumult of battle, there may be seeming disorder and yet no real disorder at all; amid

confusion and chaos, your array may be without head or tail, yet it will be proof against defeat.

17. Simulated disorder postulates perfect discipline; simulated fear postulates courage; simulated weakness postulates strength.

18. Hiding order beneath the cloak of disorder is simply a question of subdivision; concealing courage under a show of timidity presupposes a fund of latent energy; masking strength with weakness is to be effected by tactical dispositions.

19. Thus one who is skillful at keeping the enemy on the move maintains deceitful appearances, according to which the enemy will act. He sacrifices something, that the enemy may snatch at it.

20. By holding out baits, he keeps him on the march; then with a body of picked men he lies in wait for him.

21. The clever combatant looks to the effect of combined energy, and does not require too much from individuals. Hence his ability to pick out the right men and utilize combined energy.

22. When he utilizes combined energy, his fighting men become as it were like unto rolling logs or stones. For it is the nature of a log or stone to remain motionless on level ground, and to move when on a slope; if four-cornered, to come to a standstill, but if round-shaped, to go rolling down.

23. Thus the energy developed by good fighting men is as the momentum of a round stone rolled down a mountain thousands of feet in height. So much on the subject of energy.

CHAPTER VI: WEAK POINTS AND STRONG

1. Sun Tzu said: Whoever is first in the field and awaits the coming of the enemy, will be fresh for the fight; whoever is second in the field and has to hasten to battle will arrive exhausted.

2. Therefore the clever combatant imposes his will on the enemy, but does not allow the enemy's will to be imposed on him.

3. By holding out advantages to him, he can cause the enemy to approach of his own accord; or, by inflicting damage, he can make it impossible for the enemy to draw near.

4. If the enemy is taking his ease, he can harass him; if well supplied with food, he can starve him out; if quietly encamped, he can force him to move.

5. Appear at points which the enemy must hasten to defend; march swiftly to places where you are not expected.

6. An army may march great distances without distress, if it marches through country where the enemy is not.

7. You can be sure of succeeding in your attacks if you only attack places which are undefended. You can ensure the safety of your defense if you only hold positions that cannot be attacked.

8. Hence that general is skillful in attack whose opponent does not know what to defend; and he is skillful in defense whose opponent does not know what to attack.

9. Oh divine art of subtlety and secrecy! Through you we learn to be invisible, through you inaudible; and hence we can hold the enemy's fate in our hands.

10. You may advance and be absolutely irresistible, if you make for the enemy's weak points. You may retire and be safe from pursuit if your movements are more rapid than those of the enemy.

11. If we wish to fight, the enemy can be forced to an engagement even though he be sheltered behind a high rampart and a deep ditch. All we need do is attack some other place that he will be obliged to relieve.

12. If we do not wish to fight, we can prevent the enemy from engaging us even though the lines of our encampment be merely traced out on the ground. All we need do is to throw something odd and unaccountable in his way.

13. By discovering the enemy's dispositions and remaining invisible ourselves, we can keep our forces concentrated, while the enemy's must be divided.

14. We can form a single united body, while the enemy must split up into fractions. Hence there will be a whole pitted against separate parts of a whole, which means that we shall be many to the enemy's few.

15. And if we are able thus to attack an inferior force with a superior one, our opponents will be in dire straits.

16. The spot where we intend to fight must not be made known, for then the enemy will have to prepare against a possible attack at several different points. And his forces being thus distributed in many directions, the numbers we shall have to face at any given point will be proportionately few.

17. For should the enemy strengthen his van, he will weaken his rear; should he strengthen his rear, he will weaken his van; should he strengthen his left, he will weaken his right; should he strengthen his right, he will weaken his left. If he sends reinforcements everywhere, he will everywhere be weak.

18. Numerical weakness comes from having to prepare against possible attacks; numerical strength, from compelling our adversary to make these preparations against us.

19. Knowing the place and the time of the coming battle, we may concentrate from the greatest distances in order to fight.

20. But if neither time nor place be known, then the left

wing will be impotent to succor the right, the right equally impotent to succor the left, the van unable to relieve the rear, or the rear to support the van. How much more so if the furthest portions of the army are anything under a hundred LI apart, and even the nearest are separated by several LI!

21. Though according to my estimate the soldiers of Yueh exceed our own in number, that shall advantage them nothing in the matter of victory. I say then that victory can be achieved.

22. Though the enemy be stronger in numbers, we may prevent him from fighting. Scheme so as to discover his plans and the likelihood of their success.

23. Rouse him, and learn the principle of his activity or inactivity. Force him to reveal himself, so as to find out his vulnerable spots.

24. Carefully compare the opposing army with your own, so that you may know where strength is superabundant and where it is deficient.

25. In making tactical dispositions, the highest pitch you can attain is to conceal them. Conceal your dispositions, and you will be safe from the prying of the subtlest spies, from the machinations of the wisest brains.

26. How victory may be produced for them out of the enemy's own tactics -- that is what the multitude cannot comprehend.

27. All men can see the tactics whereby I conquer, but what none can see is the strategy out of which victory is evolved.

28. Do not repeat the tactics which have gained you one victory, but let your methods be regulated by the infinite variety of circumstances.

29. Military tactics are like unto water, for water in its natural course runs away from high places and hastens downwards.

30. So in war, the way is to avoid what is strong and to strike at what is weak.

31. Water shapes its course according to the nature of the ground over which it flows; the soldier works out his victory in relation to the foe whom he is facing.

32. Therefore, just as water retains no constant shape, so in warfare there are no constant conditions.

33. He who can modify his tactics in relation to his opponent and thereby succeed in winning may be called a heaven-born captain.

34. The five elements (water, fire, wood, metal, earth) are not always equally predominant; the four seasons make way for each other in turn. There are short days and long; the moon has its periods of waning and waxing.

THE ART OF WAR

CHAPTER VII: MANEUVERING

1. Sun Tzu said: In war, the general receives his commands
from the sovereign.

2. Having collected an army and concentrated his forces,
he must blend and harmonize the different elements thereof
before pitching his camp.

3. After that, comes tactical maneuvering, than which there
is nothing more difficult. The difficulty of tactical
maneuvering consists in turning the devious into the direct,
and misfortune into gain.

4. Thus, to take a long and circuitous route, after enticing
the enemy out of the way, and though starting after him, to
contrive to reach the goal before him, shows knowledge of
the artifice of DEVIATION.

5. Maneuvering with an army is advantageous; with an
undisciplined multitude, most dangerous.

6. If you set a fully equipped army in march in order to
snatch an advantage, the chances are that you will be too
late. On the other hand, to detach a flying column for the
purpose involves the sacrifice of its baggage and stores.

7. Thus, if you order your men to roll up their buff-coats,
and make forced marches without halting day or night,

covering double the usual distance at a stretch, doing a hundred LI in order to wrest an advantage, the leaders of all your three divisions will fall into the hands of the enemy.

8. The stronger men will be in front, the jaded ones will fall behind, and on this plan only one-tenth of your army will reach its destination.

9. If you march fifty LI in order to outmaneuver the enemy, you will lose the leader of your first division, and only half your force will reach the goal.

10. If you march thirty LI with the same object, two-thirds of your army will arrive.

11. We may take it then that an army without its baggage-train is lost; without provisions it is lost; without bases of supply it is lost.

12. We cannot enter into alliances until we are acquainted with the designs of our neighbors.

13. We are not fit to lead an army on the march unless we are familiar with the face of the country -- its mountains and forests, its pitfalls and precipices, its marshes and swamps.

14. We shall be unable to turn natural advantage to account unless we make use of local guides.

15. In war, practice dissimulation and you will succeed.

16. Whether to concentrate or to divide your troops must be decided by circumstances.

17. Let your rapidity be that of the wind, your compactness that of the forest.

18. In raiding and plundering be like fire, immovability like a mountain.

19. Let your plans be dark and impenetrable as night, and when you move, fall like a thunderbolt.

20. When you plunder a countryside, let the spoil be divided amongst your men; when you capture new territory, cut it up into allotments for the benefit of the soldiery.

21. Ponder and deliberate before you make a move.

22. He will conquer who has learnt the artifice of deviation. Such is the art of maneuvering.

23. The Book of Army Management says: On the field of battle, the spoken word does not carry far enough: hence the institution of gongs and drums. Nor can ordinary objects be seen clearly enough, hence the institution of banners and flags.

24. Gongs and drums, banners and flags, are means whereby the ears and eyes of the host may be focused on one particular point.

25. The host thus forming a single united body, is it impossible either for the brave to advance alone, or for the cowardly to retreat alone. This is the art of handling large masses of men.

26. In night-fighting, then, make much use of signal-fires and drums, and in fighting by day, of flags and banners, as a means of influencing the ears and eyes of your army.

27. A whole army may be robbed of its spirit; a commander-in-chief may be robbed of his presence of mind.

28. Now a soldier's spirit is keenest in the morning; by noonday it has begun to flag; and in the evening, his mind is bent only on returning to camp.

29. A clever general, therefore, avoids an army when its spirit is keen, but attacks it when it is sluggish and inclined to return. This is the art of studying moods.

30. Disciplined and calm, to await the appearance of disorder and hubbub amongst the enemy -- this is the art of retaining self-possession.

31. To be near the goal while the enemy is still far from it, to wait at ease while the enemy is toiling and struggling, to be well-fed while the enemy is famished -- this is the art of husbanding one's strength.

32. To refrain from intercepting an enemy whose banners

are in perfect order, to refrain from attacking an army drawn up in calm and confident array -- this is the art of studying circumstances.

33. It is a military axiom not to advance uphill against the enemy, nor to oppose him when he comes downhill.

34. Do not pursue an enemy who simulates flight; do not attack soldiers whose temper is keen.

35. Do not swallow bait offered by the enemy. Do not interfere with an army that is returning home.

36. When you surround an army, leave an outlet free. Do not press a desperate foe too hard.

37. Such is the art of warfare.

THE ART OF WAR

CHAPTER VIII: VARIATION IN TACTICS

1. Sun Tzu said: In war, the general receives his commands from the sovereign, collects his army and concentrates his forces

2. When in difficult country, do not encamp. In country where high roads intersect, join hands with your allies. Do not linger in dangerously isolated positions. In hemmed-in situations, you must resort to stratagem. In desperate position, you must fight.

3. There are roads which must not be followed, armies which must be not attacked, towns which must not be besieged, positions which must not be contested, commands of the sovereign which must not be obeyed.

4. The general who thoroughly understands the advantages that accompany variation of tactics knows how to handle his troops.

5. The general who does not understand these, may be well acquainted with the configuration of the country, yet he will not be able to turn his knowledge to practical account.

6. So, the student of war who is unversed in the art of war of varying his plans, even though he be acquainted with the Five Advantages, will fail to make the best use of his men.

7. Hence in the wise leader's plans, considerations of advantage and of disadvantage will be blended together.

8. If our expectation of advantage be tempered in this way, we may succeed in accomplishing the essential part of our schemes.

9. If, on the other hand, in the midst of difficulties we are always ready to seize an advantage, we may extricate ourselves from misfortune.

10. Reduce the hostile chiefs by inflicting damage on them and make trouble for them, and keep them constantly engaged; hold out specious allurements, and make them rush to any given point.

11. The art of war teaches us to rely not on the likelihood of the enemy's not coming, but on our own readiness to receive him; not on the chance of his not attacking, but rather on the fact that we have made our position unassailable.

12. There are five dangerous faults which may affect a general:

(1) Recklessness, which leads to destruction;
(2) Cowardice, which leads to capture;
(3) A hasty temper, which can be provoked by insults;
(4) A delicacy of honor which is sensitive to shame;
(5) Over-solicitude for his men, which exposes him to worry and trouble.

13. These are the five besetting sins of a general, ruinous to the conduct of war.

14. When an army is overthrown and its leader slain, the cause will surely be found among these five dangerous faults. Let them be a subject of meditation.

THE ART OF WAR

CHAPTER IX: THE ARMY ON THE MARCH

1. Sun Tzu said: We come now to the question of encamping the army and observing signs of the enemy. Pass quickly over mountains, and keep in the neighborhood of valleys.

2. Camp in high places, facing the sun. Do not climb heights in order to fight. So much for mountain warfare.

3. After crossing a river, you should get far away from it.

4. When an invading force crosses a river in its onward march, do not advance to meet it in mid-stream. It will be best to let half the army get across, and then deliver your attack.

5. If you are anxious to fight, you should not go to meet the invader near a river which he has to cross.

6. Moor your craft higher up than the enemy, and facing the sun. Do not move up-stream to meet the enemy. So much for river warfare.

7. In crossing salt-marshes, your sole concern should be to get over them quickly, without any delay.

8. If forced to fight in a salt-marsh, you should have water and grass near you, and get your back to a clump of trees.

So much for operations in salt-marches.

9. In dry, level country, take up an easily accessible position with rising ground to your right and on your rear, so that the danger may be in front, and safety lie behind. So much for campaigning in flat country.

10. These are the four useful branches of military knowledge which enabled the Yellow Emperor to vanquish four several sovereigns.

11. All armies prefer high ground to low and sunny places to dark.

12. If you are careful of your men, and camp on hard ground, the army will be free from disease of every kind, and this will spell victory.

13. When you come to a hill or a bank, occupy the sunny side, with the slope on your right rear. Thus you will at once act for the benefit of your soldiers and utilize the natural advantages of the ground.

14. When, in consequence of heavy rains up-country, a river which you wish to ford is swollen and flecked with foam, you must wait until it subsides.

15. Country in which there are precipitous cliffs with torrents running between, deep natural hollows, confined places, tangled thickets, quagmires and crevasses, should be left with all possible speed and not approached.

16. While we keep away from such places, we should get the enemy to approach them; while we face them, we should let the enemy have them on his rear.

17. If in the neighborhood of your camp there should be any hilly country, ponds surrounded by aquatic grass, hollow basins filled with reeds, or woods with thick undergrowth, they must be carefully routed out and searched; for these are places where men in ambush or insidious spies are likely to be lurking.

18. When the enemy is close at hand and remains quiet, he is relying on the natural strength of his position.

19. When he keeps aloof and tries to provoke a battle, he is anxious for the other side to advance.

20. If his place of encampment is easy of access, he is tendering a bait.

21. Movement amongst the trees of a forest shows that the enemy is advancing. The appearance of a number of screens in the midst of thick grass means that the enemy wants to make us suspicious.

22. The rising of birds in their flight is the sign of an ambuscade. Startled beasts indicate that a sudden attack is coming.

23. When there is dust rising in a high column, it is the sign of chariots advancing; when the dust is low, but spread over a wide area, it betokens the approach of infantry.

When it branches out in different directions, it shows that parties have been sent to collect firewood. A few clouds of dust moving to and fro signify that the army is encamping.

24. Humble words and increased preparations are signs that the enemy is about to advance. Violent language and driving forward as if to the attack are signs that he will retreat.

25. When the light chariots come out first and take up a position on the wings, it is a sign that the enemy is forming for battle.

26. Peace proposals unaccompanied by a sworn covenant indicate a plot.

27. When there is much running about and the soldiers fall into rank, it means that the critical moment has come.

28. When some are seen advancing and some retreating, it is a lure.

29. When the soldiers stand leaning on their spears, they are faint from want of food.

30. If those who are sent to draw water begin by drinking themselves, the army is suffering from thirst.

31. If the enemy sees an advantage to be gained and makes no effort to secure it, the soldiers are exhausted.

32. If birds gather on any spot, it is unoccupied. Clamor by

night betokens nervousness.

33. If there is disturbance in the camp, the general's authority is weak. If the banners and flags are shifted about, sedition is afoot. If the officers are angry, it means that the men are weary.

34. When an army feeds its horses with grain and kills its cattle for food, and when the men do not hang their cooking-pots over the camp-fires, showing that they will not return to their tents, you may know that they are determined to fight to the death.

35. The sight of men whispering together in small knots or speaking in subdued tones points to disaffection amongst the rank and file.

36. Too frequent rewards signify that the enemy is at the end of his resources; too many punishments betray a condition of dire distress.

37. To begin by bluster, but afterwards to take fright at the enemy's numbers, shows a supreme lack of intelligence.

38. When envoys are sent with compliments in their mouths, it is a sign that the enemy wishes for a truce.

39. If the enemy's troops march up angrily and remain facing ours for a long time without either joining battle or taking themselves off again, the situation is one that demands great vigilance and circumspection.

40. If our troops are no more in number than the enemy, that is amply sufficient; it only means that no direct attack can be made. What we can do is simply to concentrate all our available strength, keep a close watch on the enemy, and obtain reinforcements.

41. He who exercises no forethought but makes light of his opponents is sure to be captured by them.

42. If soldiers are punished before they have grown attached to you, they will not prove submissive, and unless submissive, then will be practically useless. If, when the soldiers have become attached to you, punishments are not enforced, they will still be useless.

43. Therefore soldiers must be treated in the first instance with humanity, but kept under control by means of iron discipline. This is a certain road to victory.

44. If in training soldiers commands are habitually enforced, the army will be well-disciplined; if not, its discipline will be bad.

45. If a general shows confidence in his men but always insists on his orders being obeyed, the gain will be mutual.

CHAPTER X: TERRAIN

1. Sun Tzu said: We may distinguish six kinds of terrain, to wit: (1) Accessible ground; (2) entangling ground; (3) temporizing ground; (4) narrow passes; (5) precipitous heights; (6) positions at a great distance from the enemy.

2. Ground which can be freely traversed by both sides is called accessible.

3. With regard to ground of this nature, be before the enemy in occupying the raised and sunny spots, and carefully guard your line of supplies. Then you will be able to fight with advantage.

4. Ground which can be abandoned but is hard to re-occupy is called entangling.

5. From a position of this sort, if the enemy is unprepared, you may sally forth and defeat him. But if the enemy is prepared for your coming, and you fail to defeat him, then, return being impossible, disaster will ensue.

6. When the position is such that neither side will gain by making the first move, it is called temporizing ground.

7. In a position of this sort, even though the enemy should offer us an attractive bait, it will be advisable not to stir forth, but rather to retreat, thus enticing the enemy in his turn; then, when part of his army has come out, we may

deliver our attack with advantage.

8. With regard to narrow passes, if you can occupy them first, let them be strongly garrisoned and await the advent of the enemy.

9. Should the army forestall you in occupying a pass, do not go after him if the pass is fully garrisoned, but only if it is weakly garrisoned.

10. With regard to precipitous heights, if you are beforehand with your adversary, you should occupy the raised and sunny spots, and there wait for him to come up.

11. If the enemy has occupied them before you, do not follow him, but retreat and try to entice him away.

12. If you are situated at a great distance from the enemy and the strength of the two armies is equal, it is not easy to provoke a battle, and fighting will be to your disadvantage.

13. These six are the principles connected with Earth. The general who has attained a responsible post must be careful to study them.

14. Now an army is exposed to six several calamities, not arising from natural causes, but from faults for which the general is responsible. These are: (1) Flight; (2) insubordination; (3) collapse; (4) ruin; (5) disorganization; (6) rout.

15. Other conditions being equal, if one force is hurled

against another ten times its size, the result will be the flight of the former.

16. When the common soldiers are too strong and their officers too weak, the result is insubordination. When the officers are too strong and the common soldiers too weak, the result is collapse.

17. When the higher officers are angry and insubordinate, and on meeting the enemy give battle on their own account from a feeling of resentment, before the commander-in-chief can tell whether or not he is in a position to fight, the result is ruin.

18. When the general is weak and without authority; when his orders are not clear and distinct; when there are no fixes duties assigned to officers and men, and the ranks are formed in a slovenly haphazard manner, the result is utter disorganization.

19. When a general, unable to estimate the enemy's strength, allows an inferior force to engage a larger one, or hurls a weak detachment against a powerful one, and neglects to place picked soldiers in the front rank, the result must be rout.

20. These are six ways of courting defeat, which must be carefully noted by the general who has attained a responsible post.

21. The natural formation of the country is the soldier's best ally; but a power of estimating the adversary, of

controlling the forces of victory, and of shrewdly calculating difficulties, dangers and distances, constitutes the test of a great general.

22. He who knows these things, and in fighting puts his knowledge into practice, will win his battles. He who knows them not, nor practices them, will surely be defeated.

23. If fighting is sure to result in victory, then you must fight, even though the ruler forbids it; if fighting will not result in victory, then you must not fight even at the ruler's bidding.

24. The general who advances without coveting fame and retreats without fearing disgrace, whose only thought is to protect his country and do good service for his sovereign, is the jewel of the kingdom.

25. Regard your soldiers as your children, and they will follow you into the deepest valleys; look upon them as your own beloved sons, and they will stand by you even unto death.

26. If, however, you are indulgent, but unable to make your authority felt; kind-hearted, but unable to enforce your commands; and incapable, moreover, of quelling disorder: then your soldiers must be likened to spoilt children. They are useless for any practical purpose.

27. If we know that our own men are in a condition to attack, but are unaware that the enemy is not open to

attack, we have gone only halfway towards victory.

28. If we know that the enemy is open to attack, but are unaware that our own men are not in a condition to attack, we have gone only halfway towards victory.

29. If we know that the enemy is open to attack, and also know that our men are in a condition to attack, but are unaware that the nature of the ground makes fighting impracticable, we have still gone only halfway towards victory.

30. Hence the experienced soldier, once in motion, is never bewildered; once he has broken camp, he is never at a loss.

31. Hence the saying: If you know the enemy and know yourself, your victory will not stand in doubt; if you know Heaven and know Earth, you may make your victory complete.

THE ART OF WAR

CHAPTER XI: THE NINE SITUATIONS

1. Sun Tzu said: The art of war recognizes nine varieties of ground: (1) Dispersive ground; (2) facile ground; (3) contentious ground; (4) open ground; (5) ground of intersecting highways; (6) serious ground; (7) difficult ground; (8) hemmed-in ground; (9) desperate ground.

2. When a chieftain is fighting in his own territory, it is dispersive ground.

3. When he has penetrated into hostile territory, but to no great distance, it is facile ground.

4. Ground, the possession of which imports great advantage to either side, is contentious ground.

5. Ground on which each side has liberty of movement is open ground.

6. Ground which forms the key to three contiguous states, so that he who occupies it first has most of the Empire at his command, is a ground of intersecting highways.

7. When an army has penetrated into the heart of a hostile country, leaving a number of fortified cities in its rear, it is serious ground.

8. Mountain forests, rugged steeps, marshes and fens -- all

country that is hard to traverse: this is difficult ground.

9. Ground which is reached through narrow gorges and from which we can only retire by tortuous paths, so that a small number of the enemy would suffice to crush a large body of our men: this is hemmed-in ground.

10. Ground on which we can only be saved from destruction by fighting without delay, is desperate ground.

11. On dispersive ground, therefore, fight not. On facile ground, halt not. On contentious ground, attack not.

12. On open ground, do not try to block the enemy's way. On the ground of intersecting highways, join hands with your allies.

13. On serious ground, gather in plunder. In difficult ground, keep steadily on the march.

14. On hemmed-in ground, resort to stratagem. On desperate ground, fight.

15. Those who were called skillful leaders of old knew how to drive a wedge between the enemy's front and rear; to prevent co-operation between his large and small divisions; to hinder the good troops from rescuing the bad, the officers from rallying their men.

16. When the enemy's men were united, they managed to keep them in disorder.

17. When it was to their advantage, they made a forward move; when otherwise, they stopped still.

18. If asked how to cope with a great host of the enemy in orderly array and on the point of marching to the attack, I should say: "Begin by seizing something which your opponent holds dear; then he will be amenable to your will."

19. Rapidity is the essence of war: take advantage of the enemy's unreadiness, make your way by unexpected routes, and attack unguarded spots.

20. The following are the principles to be observed by an invading force: The further you penetrate into a country, the greater will be the solidarity of your troops, and thus the defenders will not prevail against you.

21. Make forays in fertile country in order to supply your army with food.

22. Carefully study the well-being of your men, and do not overtax them. Concentrate your energy and hoard your strength. Keep your army continually on the move, and devise unfathomable plans.

23. Throw your soldiers into positions whence there is no escape, and they will prefer death to flight. If they will face death, there is nothing they may not achieve. Officers and men alike will put forth their uttermost strength.

24. Soldiers when in desperate straits lose the sense of fear.

If there is no place of refuge, they will stand firm. If they are in hostile country, they will show a stubborn front. If there is no help for it, they will fight hard.

25. Thus, without waiting to be marshaled, the soldiers will be constantly on the qui vive; without waiting to be asked, they will do your will; without restrictions, they will be faithful; without giving orders, they can be trusted.

26. Prohibit the taking of omens, and do away with superstitious doubts. Then, until death itself comes, no calamity need be feared.

27. If our soldiers are not overburdened with money, it is not because they have a distaste for riches; if their lives are not unduly long, it is not because they are disinclined to longevity.

28. On the day they are ordered out to battle, your soldiers may weep, those sitting up bedewing their garments, and those lying down letting the tears run down their cheeks. But let them once be brought to bay, and they will display the courage of a Chu or a Kuei.

29. The skillful tactician may be likened to the shuai-jan. Now the shuai-jan is a snake that is found in the ChUng mountains. Strike at its head, and you will be attacked by its tail; strike at its tail, and you will be attacked by its head; strike at its middle, and you will be attacked by head and tail both.

30. Asked if an army can be made to imitate the shuai-jan,

I should answer, Yes. For the men of Wu and the men of Yueh are enemies; yet if they are crossing a river in the same boat and are caught by a storm, they will come to each other's assistance just as the left hand helps the right.

31. Hence it is not enough to put one's trust in the tethering of horses, and the burying of chariot wheels in the ground.

32. The principle on which to manage an army is to set up one standard of courage which all must reach.

33. How to make the best of both strong and weak -- that is a question involving the proper use of ground.

34. Thus the skillful general conducts his army just as though he were leading a single man, willy-nilly, by the hand.

35. It is the business of a general to be quiet and thus ensure secrecy; upright and just, and thus maintain order.

36. He must be able to mystify his officers and men by false reports and appearances, and thus keep them in total ignorance.

37. By altering his arrangements and changing his plans, he keeps the enemy without definite knowledge. By shifting his camp and taking circuitous routes, he prevents the enemy from anticipating his purpose.

38. At the critical moment, the leader of an army acts like one who has climbed up a height and then kicks away the

ladder behind him. He carries his men deep into hostile territory before he shows his hand.

39. He burns his boats and breaks his cooking-pots; like a shepherd driving a flock of sheep, he drives his men this way and that, and nothing knows whither he is going.

40. To muster his host and bring it into danger -- this may be termed the business of the general.

41. The different measures suited to the nine varieties of ground, the expediency of aggressive or defensive tactics, and the fundamental laws of human nature: these are things that must most certainly be studied.

42. When invading hostile territory, the general principle is that penetrating deeply brings cohesion; penetrating but a short way means dispersion.

43. When you leave your own country behind, and take your army across neighborhood territory, you find yourself on critical ground. When there are means of communication on all four sides, the ground is one of intersecting highways.

44. When you penetrate deeply into a country, it is serious ground. When you penetrate but a little way, it is facile ground.

45. When you have the enemy's strongholds on your rear, and narrow passes in front, it is hemmed-in ground. When there is no place of refuge at all, it is desperate ground.

46. Therefore, on dispersive ground, I would inspire my men with unity of purpose. On facile ground, I would see that there is close connection between all parts of my army.

47. On contentious ground, I would hurry up my rear.

48. On open ground, I would keep a vigilant eye on my defenses. On ground of intersecting highways, I would consolidate my alliances.

49. On serious ground, I would try to ensure a continuous stream of supplies. On difficult ground, I would keep pushing on along the road.

50. On hemmed-in ground, I would block any way of retreat. On desperate ground, I would proclaim to my soldiers the hopelessness of saving their lives.

51. For it is the soldier's disposition to offer an obstinate resistance when surrounded, to fight hard when he cannot help himself, and to obey promptly when he has fallen into danger.

52. We cannot enter into alliance with neighboring princes until we are acquainted with their designs. We are not fit to lead an army on the march unless we are familiar with the face of the country -- its mountains and forests, its pitfalls and precipices, its marshes and swamps. We shall be unable to turn natural advantages to account unless we make use of local guides.

53. To be ignored of any one of the following four or five principles does not befit a warlike prince.

54. When a warlike prince attacks a powerful state, his generalship shows itself in preventing the concentration of the enemy's forces. He overawes his opponents, and their allies are prevented from joining against him.

55. Hence he does not strive to ally himself with all and sundry, nor does he foster the power of other states. He carries out his own secret designs, keeping his antagonists in awe. Thus he is able to capture their cities and overthrow their kingdoms.

56. Bestow rewards without regard to rule, issue orders without regard to previous arrangements; and you will be able to handle a whole army as though you had to do with but a single man.

57. Confront your soldiers with the deed itself; never let them know your design. When the outlook is bright, bring it before their eyes; but tell them nothing when the situation is gloomy.

58. Place your army in deadly peril, and it will survive; plunge it into desperate straits, and it will come off in safety.

59. For it is precisely when a force has fallen into harm's way that is capable of striking a blow for victory.

60. Success in warfare is gained by carefully

accommodating ourselves to the enemy's purpose.

61. By persistently hanging on the enemy's flank, we shall succeed in the long run in killing the commander-in-chief.

62. This is called ability to accomplish a thing by sheer cunning.

63. On the day that you take up your command, block the frontier passes, destroy the official tallies, and stop the passage of all emissaries.

64. Be stern in the council-chamber, so that you may control the situation.

65. If the enemy leaves a door open, you must rush in.

66. Forestall your opponent by seizing what he holds dear, and subtly contrive to time his arrival on the ground.

67. Walk in the path defined by rule, and accommodate yourself to the enemy until you can fight a decisive battle.

68. At first, then, exhibit the coyness of a maiden until the enemy gives you an opening; afterwards emulate the rapidity of a running hare, and it will be too late for the enemy to oppose you.

THE ART OF WAR

THE ART OF WAR

CHAPTER XII: THE ATTACK BY FIRE

1. Sun Tzu said: There are five ways of attacking with fire. The first is to burn soldiers in their camp; the second is to burn stores; the third is to burn baggage trains; the fourth is to burn arsenals and magazines; the fifth is to hurl dropping fire amongst the enemy.

2. In order to carry out an attack, we must have means available. The material for raising fire should always be kept in readiness.

3. There is a proper season for making attacks with fire, and special days for starting a conflagration.

4. The proper season is when the weather is very dry; the special days are those when the moon is in the constellations of the Sieve, the Wall, the Wing or the Cross-bar; for these four are all days of rising wind.

5. In attacking with fire, one should be prepared to meet five possible developments:

6. (1) When fire breaks out inside to enemy's camp, respond at once with an attack from without.

7. (2) If there is an outbreak of fire, but the enemy's soldiers remain quiet, bide your time and do not attack.

8. (3) When the force of the flames has reached its height, follow it up with an attack, if that is practicable; if not, stay where you are.

9. (4) If it is possible to make an assault with fire from without, do not wait for it to break out within, but deliver your attack at a favorable moment.

10. (5) When you start a fire, be to windward of it. Do not attack from the leeward.

11. A wind that rises in the daytime lasts long, but a night breeze soon falls.

12. In every army, the five developments connected with fire must be known, the movements of the stars calculated, and a watch kept for the proper days.

13. Hence those who use fire as an aid to the attack show intelligence; those who use water as an aid to the attack gain an accession of strength.

14. By means of water, an enemy may be intercepted, but not robbed of all his belongings.

15. Unhappy is the fate of one who tries to win his battles and succeed in his attacks without cultivating the spirit of enterprise; for the result is waste of time and general stagnation.

16. Hence the saying: The enlightened ruler lays his plans well ahead; the good general cultivates his resources.

17. Move not unless you see an advantage; use not your troops unless there is something to be gained; fight not unless the position is critical.

18. No ruler should put troops into the field merely to gratify his own spleen; no general should fight a battle simply out of pique.

19. If it is to your advantage, make a forward move; if not, stay where you are.

20. Anger may in time change to gladness; vexation may be succeeded by content.

21. But a kingdom that has once been destroyed can never come again into being; nor can the dead ever be brought back to life.

22. Hence the enlightened ruler is heedful, and the good general full of caution. This is the way to keep a country at peace and an army intact.

THE ART OF WAR

CHAPTER XIII: THE USE OF SPIES

1. Sun Tzu said: Raising a host of a hundred thousand men and marching them great distances entails heavy loss on the people and a drain on the resources of the State. The daily expenditure will amount to a thousand ounces of silver. There will be commotion at home and abroad, and men will drop down exhausted on the highways. As many as seven hundred thousand families will be impeded in their labor.

2. Hostile armies may face each other for years, striving for the victory which is decided in a single day. This being so, to remain in ignorance of the enemy's condition simply because one grudges the outlay of a hundred ounces of silver in honors and emoluments, is the height of inhumanity.

3. One who acts thus is no leader of men, no present help to his sovereign, no master of victory.

4. Thus, what enables the wise sovereign and the good general to strike and conquer, and achieve things beyond the reach of ordinary men, is foreknowledge.

5. Now this foreknowledge cannot be elicited from spirits; it cannot be obtained inductively from experience, nor by any deductive calculation.

6. Knowledge of the enemy's dispositions can only be

obtained from other men.

7. Hence the use of spies, of whom there are five classes: (1) local spies; (2) inward spies; (3) converted spies; (4) doomed spies; (5) surviving spies.

8. When these five kinds of spy are all at work, none can discover the secret system. This is called "divine manipulation of the threads." It is the sovereign's most precious faculty.

9. Having local spies means employing the services of the inhabitants of a district.

10. Having inward spies, making use of officials of the enemy.

11. Having converted spies, getting hold of the enemy's spies and using them for our own purposes.

12. Having doomed spies, doing certain things openly for purposes of deception, and allowing our spies to know of them and report them to the enemy.

13. Surviving spies, finally, are those who bring back news from the enemy's camp.

14. Hence it is that which none in the whole army are more intimate relations to be maintained than with spies. None should be more liberally rewarded. In no other business should greater secrecy be preserved.

15. Spies cannot be usefully employed without a certain intuitive sagacity.

16. They cannot be properly managed without benevolence and straightforwardness.

17. Without subtle ingenuity of mind, one cannot make certain of the truth of their reports.

18. Be subtle! Be subtle, and use your spies for every kind of business.

19. If a secret piece of news is divulged by a spy before the time is ripe, he must be put to death together with the man to whom the secret was told.

20. Whether the object be to crush an army, to storm a city, or to assassinate an individual, it is always necessary to begin by finding out the names of the attendants, the aides-de-camp, and door-keepers and sentries of the general in command. Our spies must be commissioned to ascertain these.

21. The enemy's spies who have come to spy on us must be sought out, tempted with bribes, led away and comfortably housed. Thus they will become converted spies and available for our service.

22. It is through the information brought by the converted spy that we are able to acquire and employ local and inward spies.

23. It is owing to his information, again, that we can cause the doomed spy to carry false tidings to the enemy.

24. Lastly, it is by his information that the surviving spy can be used on appointed occasions.

25. The end and aim of spying in all its five varieties is knowledge of the enemy; and this knowledge can only be derived, in the first instance, from the converted spy. Hence it is essential that the converted spy be treated with the utmost liberality.

26. Of old, the rise of the Yin dynasty was due to I Chih who had served under the Hsia. Likewise, the rise of the Chou dynasty was due to Lu Ya who had served under the Yin.

27. Hence it is only the enlightened ruler and the wise general who will use the highest intelligence of the army for purposes of spying and thereby achieve great results. Spies are a most important element in water, because on them depends an army's ability to move.

A Book of Five Rings
(Go Rin No Sho)

Written by Miyamoto Musashi

Translated by D.W.

A BOOK OF FIVE RINGS

Introduction

It is now during the first ten days of the tenth month in the twentieth year of Kanei (1645). I am sixty years old and I have been training many years in the Way of strategy called Ni Ten Ichi Ryu. I will now explain it in writing for the first time. I have climbed mountain Iwato of Higo in Kyushu to pray to Kwannon and kneel before Buddha. I am a warrior of Harima province, Shinmen Musashi No Kami Fujiwara No Geshin.

Since I was a youth my heart has been drawn toward the Way of strategy. My first duel took place at age thirteen when I struck down a strategist of the Shinto school, one Arima Kihei. I was sixteen when I struck down an able strategist, Tadashima Akiyama, and when I was twenty-one I went up to the capital and met all manner of strategists, never once failing to win in many contests. After that I went from province to province, dueling with strategists of various schools, and not once did I fail to win though I had as many as sixty encounters.

When I reached age thirty I looked back on my past and realized the previous victories were not due to my having mastered strategy. Perhaps they resulted from natural ability, or the order of heaven, or in that other schools' strategy was inferior. After this I studied morning and evening searching for the principle, and came to realize the Way of strategy when I was fifty.

Since then I have lived without following any particular Way. Thus with the virtue of strategy I can now practice many arts and abilities without the need for a teacher. In writing this book I did not use the law of Buddha or the teachings of Confucius, neither old war chronicles nor books on martial tactics. My purpose in writing is to explain the true spirit of this Ichi School as it is mirrored in the Way of heaven and Kwannon.

The time is the night of the tenth day of the tenth month, at the hour of the tiger (3-5 a.m.)

The Ground Book

Strategy is the craft of the warrior. Commanders must enact the craft, and troopers should know this Way. There is no warrior in the world today that really understands the Way of strategy.

There are various Ways. There is the Way of salvation by the law of Buddha, the Way of Confucius governing the Way of learning, the Way of healing as a doctor, the Way of Waka teaching as a poet, as well as tea, archery, and many arts and skills. Every man should practice as he feels inclined.

It is said that the warrior's way is the twofold Way of pen and sword, and he should have a taste for both Ways. Even if a man has no natural ability, he can be a warrior by sticking assiduously to both divisions of the Way. Generally speaking, the Way of the warrior is to determinedly accept death. Although others (women, peasants and lowlier folk) have been known to die readily in the cause of duty or out of shame, the warrior is different. The warrior is different in that studying the Way of strategy is based on overcoming men. By winning in crossing swords with individuals, or enjoining battle with large numbers, the warrior attains power and fame for himself and for his lord. This is the virtue of strategy.

The Way of Strategy

In China and Japan practitioners of the Way have been known as "masters of strategy". Warriors must learn this Way.

Recently there have been people claiming to be strategists, but they are usually just sword-fencers. In olden times, strategy was listed among the Ten Abilities and Seven Arts as a beneficial practice. Strategy was certainly an art but as a beneficial practice it was not limited only to sword fencing. Indeed, the true value of sword fencing cannot be seen within the confines of sword-fencing technique.

If we look at the world we see that men use equipment to sell themselves. In this type of Way of strategy, they are looking for profit, and both those teaching and those learning the way are concerned with coloring and showing off their technique. Someone once said "Immature strategy is the cause of grief". That was a true saying.

There are four Ways in which men pass through life: as gentlemen, farmers, artisans and merchants.

First is the way of the farmer. Using agricultural instruments, he sees springs through to autumns with an eye on the changes of season.

Second is the Way of the merchant. The wine maker obtains his ingredients and puts them to use to make his living. The Way of the merchant is always to live by taking profit.

Third is the gentleman warrior, carrying the weaponry of his Way. The Way of the warrior is to master the virtue of his weapons. He must have a leaning toward strategy, for if a gentleman dislikes strategy he will not appreciate the benefit of weaponry.

Fourth is the Way of the artisan. The Way of the carpenter is to become proficient in the use of his tools, first to lay his plans with a true measure and then perform his work according to plan. Thus he passes through life.

These are the four Ways of the gentleman, the farmer, the artisan and the merchant.

Comparing the Way of the Carpenter to Strategy

The comparison with carpentry is through the connection with houses. The carpenter uses a master plan of the building, and the Way of strategy is similar in this manner of planning. If you want to learn the craft of war, study this book with a view of the teacher as a needle, the disciple as thread. You must practice constantly.

Like the foreman carpenter, the commander must know natural rules, and the rules of the country, and the rules of houses. This is the Way of the foreman.
The foreman carpenter must know the architectural theory of towers and temples, the plans of palaces, and must employ men to build houses. The Way of the foreman

carpenter is the same as the Way of the commander of a warrior house.

In the construction of houses, one must choose the wood. Straight, unknotted timber of good appearance is used for revealed pillars; straight timber with small defects is used for the inner pillars. Timber of the finest appearance, even if a little weak, is used for the thresholds, lintels, doors, sliding doors, and so on. Good strong timber, though it be gnarled and knotted, can always be used discreetly in construction. Timber which is weak or knotted throughout should be used as scaffolding, and later for firewood.

The foreman carpenter allots his men work according to their ability. Floor layers, makers of sliding doors, thresholds and lintels, ceilings and so on. Those of poor ability lay the floor joist, and those of lesser ability carve wedges and do such miscellaneous work. If the foreman knows and deploys his men well, the finished work will be good.

The foreman should take into account the abilities and limitations of his men, circulating among them and asking nothing unreasonable. He should know their morale and spirit, and encourage them when necessary. This is the same as the principle of strategy.

The Way of Strategy

Like a trooper, the carpenter sharpens his own tools. He carries his equipment in his toolbox, and works under the direction of his foreman. He makes columns and girders with an axe, shapes floorboards and shelves with a plane, cuts fine openwork and carvings accurately, giving as excellent a finish as his skill will allow. This is the craft of carpenters. When the carpenter becomes skilled and understands measures, he can become a foreman. These are the specialties of the carpenter. Things are similar for the trooper. You ought to think deeply about this.

The attainment of the carpenter is that his work is not warped, that the joints are not misaligned, and that the work is truly planed so that it meets well and is not merely finished in sections. This is essential.

If you want to learn this Way, deeply consider the things written in this book one at a time. You must do sufficient research.

Outline of the Five Books of this Book of Strategy

The Way is shown in five books concerning different aspects. These books are Ground, Water, Fire, Tradition (Wind) and Void.

In the Ground book, the body of the Way of strategy is explained from the viewpoint of my Ichi School. The true Way is not realized through sword fencing alone. One must know the smallest things and the biggest things, the shallowest things and the deepest things. As if it were a straight road mapped out on the ground, the first book is called the Ground book.

Second is the Water book. With water as the basis, the spirit becomes like water. Water adopts the shape of its receptacle; sometimes it is a trickle, sometimes a wild sea. Water has a clear blue color, and through its clarity the truths of my Ichi School are revealed in this book.

If you master the principles of sword fencing, when you freely beat one man, you can beat any man in the world. The spirit of defeating a man is the same for ten million men. The accomplished strategist makes small things into big things; the principle of strategy is that knowing one thing is to know ten thousand things. I cannot write in detail how this is done.

Third is the Fire book. This book is about fighting. The spirit of fire is fierce whether the fire be small or big; and so it is with battles. The Way of battles is the same for fights between two men as for ten thousand to-a-side battles. You must appreciate that spirit can become big or small. What is big is easy to perceive; what is small is difficult to perceive. In short, it is difficult for large numbers of men to change position, so their movements can be easily predicted. An individual can easily change his mind, so his movements are difficult to predict. It is important to grasp this.

The core of this book is that you must train day and night in order to make quick decisions. Strategy entails treating training as a part of normal life with your spirit unchanging. Thus combat in battle is described in the Fire book.

Fourth is the Wind book. This book is not concerned with the Ichi School but with other schools of strategy. By Wind I mean old traditions, present-day traditions, and family traditions of strategy. Thus I clearly explain the strategies of the world. It is difficult to know yourself if you do not know others.

There are sidetracks to all Ways. If you study a Way daily, and your spirit diverges, you may think you are obeying a good way, but objectively it is not the true Way. If you are following the true Way and diverge a little, this will later become a large divergence.

Other strategies have come to be thought of as mere sword fencing, however the benefit of my strategy, although it includes sword fencing, lies in a separate principle. Thus I explain what is commonly meant by strategy in other schools in the Tradition (Wind) book.

Fifth is the book of the Void. By Void I mean that which has no beginning and no end. Attaining this principle means not attaining the principle. The Way of strategy is the Way of nature. When you appreciate the power of nature and are in tune with the rhythm of any situation, you will be able to hit the enemy naturally and strike naturally. All this is the Way of the Void. I intend to show how to follow the true Way according to nature in the book of the Void.

The Name Ichi Ryu Ni To (One school - Two swords)

Warriors, both commanders and troopers, carry two swords at their belt. In the olden days these were called the long sword and the sword; nowadays they are known as the sword and the companion sword. "Nito Ichi Ryu" shows the advantage of using both swords.

Students of the Ichi School Way of strategy should train from the start with the sword and long sword in either hand. This is the truth: when you sacrifice your life, you must make fullest use of your weaponry. Not to do so, and to die with a weapon not yet drawn, is false.

If you hold a sword with both hands, it is difficult to wield it freely to left and right, so my method is to carry the sword in one hand. This does not apply to large weapons such as the spear or halberd (weapons that are carried out of doors), but swords and companion swords can be carried in one hand. It is encumbering to hold a sword in both hands when you are on horseback, when running on uneven roads, on swampy ground, muddy rice fields, stony ground, or in a crowd of people. To hold the long sword in both hands is not the true Way, for if you carry a bow or spear or other arms in your left hand you have only one hand free for the long sword.

However, when it is difficult to cut an enemy down with one hand, you must use both hands. It is not difficult to wield a sword in one hand; the Way to learn this is to train with two long swords, one in each hand. It will seem difficult at first, but everything is difficult at first. Note that bows are difficult to draw, halberds are difficult to wield; as you become accustomed to the bow so your pull will become stronger. When you become used to wielding the long sword, you will gain the power of the Way and wield the sword well.

As I will explain in the second book, the Water Book, there is no fast way of wielding the long sword. The long sword should be wielded broadly, and the companion sword closely. This is the first thing to learn.

According to the Ichi School, you can win with a long or with a short weapon. The Way of the Ichi School is the spirit of winning, whatever the weapon and whatever its size.

It is better to use two swords rather than one when you are fighting a crowd and especially if you want to take a prisoner. These things are difficult to explain in detail, but when you attain the Way of strategy there will not be anything you cannot see; from one thing, you will know ten thousand things. You must study hard.

The Benefit of the Two Characters reading "Strategy"

Masters of the long sword are called strategists. As for the other military arts, those who master the bow are called archers, those who master the spear are called spearmen, those who master the gun are called marksmen, and those who master the halberd are called halberdiers. But we do not call masters of the Way of the long sword "longswordsmen", or "companionswordsmen".

Bows, guns, spears and halberds are all warriors' equipment and they are certainly part of strategy. However, to master the virtue of the long sword is to govern the world and oneself; thus the long sword is the basis of strategy. The principle is "strategy by means of the long sword". If one attains the virtue of the long sword, one man can beat ten men. As one man can beat ten, so a hundred men can beat a thousand, and a thousand men can beat ten thousand. In my strategy, one man is the same as ten thousand, so this strategy is the complete warrior's craft.

The Way of the warrior does not include other Ways, such as Confucianism, Buddhism, certain traditions, artistic accomplishments and sword dancing. But even though these are not part of the Way, if you know the Way broadly you will see it in everything. Men must polish their particular Way.

The Benefit of Weapons in Strategy

There is a time and a place for use of weapons. The best use of the companion sword is in a confined space, or when you are engaged closely with an opponent. The long sword can be used effectively in all situations. The halberd is inferior to the spear on the battlefield. With the spear you can take the initiative; the halberd is defensive. In the hands of one of two men of equal ability, the spear gives a little extra strength. Spear and halberd both have their uses, but neither is very beneficial in confined spaces. They cannot be used for taking a prisoner. They are essentially weapons for the field.

If you learn "indoor" techniques, you will think narrowly and forget the true Way. Then you will have difficulty in actual encounters.

The bow is tactically strong at the commencement of battle, especially battles on a moor, as it is possible to shoot quickly from among the spearmen. However, it is unsatisfactory in sieges, or when the enemy is more than forty yards away. For this reason there are now few traditional schools of archery and there is little use nowadays for this kind of skill.

From inside fortifications, the gun has no equal among weapons. It is the supreme weapon on the field before the ranks clash, but once swords are crossed the gun becomes useless.

One of the virtues of the bow is that you can see the arrows in flight and correct your aim accordingly, whereas gunshot cannot be seen. You must appreciate the importance of this difference.

Weapons should be enduring and without defects. Swords and companion swords should cut strongly. Spears and halberds must stand up to heavy use. Bows and guns must be sturdy. Weapons should be hardy rather than decorative.

You should not have a favorite weapon, nor likes and dislikes. To become over-familiar with one weapon is as much a fault as not knowing it sufficiently well. You should not copy others, but use those weapons you can handle properly. These are things you must know completely.

Timing in strategy

There is timing in everything. Timing in strategy cannot be mastered without a great deal of practice.

Just as timing is important in dancing and pipe or string music - as they are in rhythm only if timing is good - timing and rhythm are also involved in the military arts, shooting bows and guns, and riding horses. In fact, all skills and abilities involve timing, and there is also timing in the Void.

There is timing in the whole life of the warrior, in his thriving and declining, in his harmony and discord. Similarly, there is timing in the Way of the merchant, in the rise and fall of capital. All things entail rising and falling timing. You must be able to discern this.

In strategy there are various timing considerations. To begin you must know the applicable timing and the inapplicable timing, the fast and slow timings, and find the relevant timing from among large and small things. Studying timing is an essential thing in strategy. It is especially important to know the background timing, otherwise your strategy will become uncertain.

You win in battles with the timing of cunning by knowing the enemies' timing, and using a timing which the enemy does not expect. All the five books are chiefly concerned with timing. You must train sufficiently to appreciate all this.

If you practice day and night in the above Ichi School strategy, your spirit will naturally broaden. This Way of strategy is recorded for the first time in the five books of Ground, Water, Fire, Tradition (Wind), and Void.

For men who want to learn my strategy, this is the Way:

- Do not think dishonestly.
- The Way is in training.
- Become acquainted with every art.
- Know the Ways of all professions.
- Distinguish between gain and loss in worldly matters.
- Develop intuitive judgment and understanding for everything.
- Perceive those things that cannot be seen.
- Pay attention even to trifles.
- Do nothing useless

It is important to start by setting these broad principles in your heart. You must train in the Way of strategy. If you do not look at things on a large scale, it will be difficult for you to master strategy; however if you learn and attain this strategy, you will never lose even to twenty or thirty enemies.

More than anything, you must set your heart on strategy and earnestly stick to the Way. By training you will be able to freely control your own body, conquer men with your body, and with sufficient training you will be able to beat men in fights, be able to win with your eye, and beat ten men with your spirit. When you have reached this point, will it not mean that you are invincible?

Further, in large scale strategy the superior man will manage many subordinates dexterously, bear himself correctly, govern the country and foster the people, thus preserving the ruler's discipline. Hence following the Way of strategy involves the spirit not being defeated, helping oneself and gaining honor.

The second year of Shoho (1645), the fifth month, the twelfth day.

A BOOK OF FIVE RINGS

The Water Book

The spirit of the Ni Ten Ichi School of strategy is based on water, and this Water Book explains methods of victory in the long-sword form of the Ichi School. While language is inadequate to explain the Way in detail, it can be grasped intuitively. Think about each word as you study this book. If you interpret the meaning loosely you will mistake the Way.

While principles of strategy are written here in terms of single combat, you must think broadly so that you attain an understanding for ten-thousand-a-side battles. Strategy is different from other things in that if you mistake the Way even a little, you will become bewildered and fall into bad ways.

You will not reach the Way of strategy by merely reading this book. This book is meant to be studied, absorbed, memorized and imitated, so that you may truly grasp its principles from within your heart and absorb them into your body.

Spiritual Bearing in Strategy

In strategy your spiritual bearing must not be any different from normal. Both in fighting and in everyday life you should be determined though calm. Meet situations without tenseness yet not recklessly, your spirit settled yet unbiased. Even when your spirit is calm do not let your body relax, and when your body is relaxed do not let your spirit slacken. Do not let your spirit be influenced by your body, nor your body be influenced by your spirit. Be neither insufficiently spirited nor over spirited. An elevated spirit is weak and a low spirit is weak. Do not let the enemy see your spirit.

Small people must be completely familiar with the spirit of large people, and large people must be familiar with the spirit of small people. Whatever your size, do not be misled by the reactions of your own body. With your spirit open and unrestricted, look at things from a high point of view. Cultivate and polish your wisdom: learn public justice, distinguish between good and evil, and study the Ways of different arts one by one. When you are not deceived by men you will have realized the wisdom of strategy.

The wisdom of strategy is different from other things. You should ceaselessly research the principles of strategy so that you can develop a steady spirit.

Stance in Strategy

Adopt a stance with the head erect, neither hanging down, nor looking up, nor twisted. Your forehead and the space between your eyes should not be wrinkled. Do not roll your eyes nor allow them to blink, rather slightly narrow them. With your features composed, keep the line of your nose straight with a feeling of slightly flaring your nostrils. Hold the line of the rear of the neck straight; instill vigor into your hairline and from the shoulders down through your entire body. Lower both shoulders and, without the buttocks jutting out, put strength into your legs from the knees to the tops of your toes. Brace your abdomen so that you do not bend at the hips. Wedge your companion sword in your belt against your abdomen, so that your belt is not slack - this is called "wedging in".

In all forms of strategy, it is necessary to maintain the combat stance in everyday life and to make your everyday stance your combat stance. You must grasp this well.

The Gaze in Strategy

The gaze should be large and broad. This is the twofold gaze - "Perception and Sight". Perception is strong and sight weak.

In strategy it is important to see distant things as if they were close and to take a distanced view of close things. It is important to know the enemy's sword and not to be distracted by insignificant movements of his sword. You must study this. The gaze is the same for single combat and for large-scale combat.

It is necessary in strategy to be able to look to both sides without moving your eyeballs. You cannot master this ability quickly. Learn what is written here: use this gaze in everyday life and never vary from it.

Holding the Long Sword

Grip the long sword with a floating feeling in your thumb and forefinger, with the middle finger neither tight nor slack, and with the last two fingers tight.
When you take up a sword, you must feel intent on cutting the enemy. As you cut an enemy you must not change your grip, and your hands must not "cower". When you dash the enemy's sword aside, or ward it off, or force it down, you must slightly change the feeling in your thumb and forefinger. Above all, you must be intent on cutting the enemy in the way you grip the sword. The grip during combat and during sword-testing is the same.

Generally, I dislike fixedness in both long swords and hands. Fixedness means a dead hand. Pliability is a living hand. You must bear this in mind.

Footwork

With the tips of your toes somewhat floating, tread firmly with your heels. Whether you move fast or slow, with large or small steps, your feet must always move as in normal walking. I dislike the three walking methods known as "jumping-foot", "floating-foot" and "fixed-steps".

So-called "Yin-Yang foot" is important to the Way. Yin-Yang foot means moving both feet; it means moving your feet left-right and right-left when cutting, withdrawing, or warding off a cut. You should not move one foot preferentially.

The Five Attitudes

There are five dimensions of attitude, and there are no attitudes but these five. The five attitudes are: Upper, Middle, Lower, Right Side, and Left Side. The one purpose of all attitudes is to cut the enemy. Whatever attitude you are in, do not be conscious of making the attitude; think only of cutting.

Your attitude should be large or small according to the situation. Upper, Lower and Middle attitudes are decisive. Left Side and Right Side attitudes are fluid. Left and Right attitudes should be used if there is an obstruction overhead or to one side. The decision to use Left or Right depends on the place.

The Middle attitude is the heart of the attitudes, the essence of the Way. To understand attitude you must thoroughly understand the Middle attitude, for if we look at strategy on a broad scale, the Middle attitude is the seat of the commander, with the other four attitudes following the commander. You must comprehend this.

The Way of the Long Sword

To know the Way of the long sword means we can wield with two fingers the sword that we usually carry. If we know the path of the sword well, we can wield it easily.

To wield the long sword well you must wield it calmly. If you try to wield the long sword quickly, like a folding fan or a short sword, you will mistake the Way and you will err by using "short sword chopping". You cannot cut a man with a long sword using this method.

When you have cut downwards with the long sword, lift it straight upwards; when you cut sideways, return the sword along a sideways path. Return the sword in a reasonable way, always stretching the elbows broadly. Wield the sword strongly. This is the Way of the long sword.

If you learn to use the five approaches of my strategy, you will be able to wield a sword well. You must train constantly.

The Five Approaches

- The first approach is the Middle attitude. Confront the enemy with the point of your sword against his face. When he attacks, dash his sword to the right and "ride" it. Or, when the enemy attacks, deflect the point of his sword by hitting downwards, keep your long sword where it is, and as the enemy renews the attack, cut his arms from below. This is the first method.

  The five approaches are similar in purpose. You must train repeatedly using a long sword in order to learn them. When you master my Way of the long sword, you will be able to control any attack the enemy makes. I assure you, there are no attitudes other than the five attitudes of the long sword of NiTo.

- In the second approach with the long sword, use the Upper attitude and cut the enemy just as he attacks. If the enemy evades the cut, keep your sword where it is and, scooping from below, cut him as he renews the attack. It is possible to repeat the cut from here.

In this method there are various changes in timing and spirit. You will be able to understand this by training in the Ichi School. You will always win with the five long sword methods. You must train repeatedly.

- In the third approach, adopt the Lower attitude, anticipating scooping up. When the enemy attacks, hit his hands from below. As you do so, he may try to hit your sword down. If this is the case, cut his upper arm(s) horizontally with a feeling of "crossing". This means that from the Lower attitudes you hit the enemy at the instant that he attacks.

You will encounter this method often, both as a beginner and in later strategy. You must train holding a long sword.

- In this fourth approach, adopt the Left Side attitude. As the enemy attacks, hit his hands from below. If as you hit his hands he attempts to dash down your sword, parry the path of his long sword with the feeling of hitting his hands and cut across from above your shoulder.

This is the Way of the long sword. Through this method you win by parrying the line of the enemy's attack. You must study this.

- In the fifth approach, the sword is in the Right Side attitude. In accordance with the enemy's attack, cross your sword from below at the side to the Upper attitude. Then cut straight from above.

  This method is essential for knowing the Way of the long sword well. If you can use this method, you can freely wield a heavy long sword.

I cannot describe in detail how to use these five approaches. You must become well acquainted with my "in harmony with the long sword" Way, learn large-scale timing, understand the enemy's long sword, and become accustomed to the five approaches. You will always win by using these five methods, with various timing considerations discerning the enemy's spirit. You must reflect upon all this carefully.

The "Attitude No-Attitude" Teaching

"Attitude No-Attitude" means that there is no need for what are known as long
sword attitudes. Even so, attitudes do exist as the five ways of holding the long sword. However you hold the sword, it must be in such a way that it is easy to cut the enemy well, in accordance with the situation, the place, and your relation to the enemy. From the Upper attitude, as your spirit lessens you can adopt the Middle attitude, and from

the Middle attitude you can raise the sword a little in your technique and adopt the Upper attitude. From the Lower attitude you can raise the sword a little and adopt the Middle attitudes as the occasion demands. According to the situation, if you turn your sword from either the Left Side or Right Side attitude towards the center, the Middle or the Lower attitude results.

This principle is known as: "Existing Attitude - Non-existing Attitude".

The most important thing when you take a sword in your hands is your intention to cut the enemy, whatever the means. Whenever you parry, hit, spring, strike or touch the enemy's cutting sword, you must cut the enemy in the same movement. This is essential. If you think only of hitting, springing, striking or touching the enemy, you will not be able actually to cut him. More than anything, you must be thinking of carrying your movement through to cutting him. To achieve this you must research it well.

Attitude in strategy on a larger scale is called "Battle Array" and is intended for winning battles. Do not use a fixed formation. Study this well.

To Hit the Enemy "In One Timing"

When you have drawn close to the enemy, hit him as quickly and directly as possible, without moving your body or settling your spirit, while you see that he is still undecided. This timing of hitting before the enemy decides to withdraw, break or hit, is called "In One Timing".

It takes training to achieve this timing and to be able to hit in the timing of an instant.

The "Abdomen Timing of Two"

When you attack and the enemy quickly retreats, as you see him tense you must feint a cut. Then, as he relaxes, follow up and hit him. This is the "Abdomen Timing of Two". It is very difficult to attain this merely by reading this book, but you will soon understand with a little instruction.

No Design, No Conception

In this method, when the enemy attacks and you decide to attack, hit with your body, hit with your spirit, and hit from the Void with your hands, accelerating strongly. This is the "No Design, No Conception" cut.

This is the most important method of hitting. It is often used. You must train hard to understand it.

The Flowing Water Cut

The "Flowing Water Cut" is used when you are struggling blade to blade with the enemy. When he breaks and quickly withdraws trying to spring with his long sword, expand your body and spirit and cut him as slowly as possible with your long sword, following your body like stagnant water. You can cut with certainty if you learn this. You must discern the enemy's grade.

The Fire and Stones Cut

The Fires and Stones Cut means that when the enemy's long sword and your long sword clash together, you cut as strongly as possible without raising the sword even a bit. This means cutting quickly with the hands, body and legs - all three cutting strongly. If you train well enough you will be able to strike strongly.

The Red Leaves Cut

The Red Leaves Cut means knocking down the enemy's long sword. When the enemy is in a long sword attitude in front of you and intent on cutting, hitting and parrying, you strongly hit the enemy's sword with the Fire and Stones Cut, perhaps in the design of the "No Design, No Conception" Cut. The spirit should be getting control of his sword. If you then beat down the point of his sword with a sticky feeling, he will necessarily drop the sword. If you practice this cut it becomes easy to make the enemy drop his sword. You must train repetitively.

The Body in Place of the Long Sword

Also called: "the long sword in place of the body". Usually we move the body and the sword at the same time to cut the enemy. However, according to the enemy's cutting method, you can dash against him with your body first, and afterwards cut with the sword. If his body is immoveable, you can cut first with the long sword, but generally you hit first with the body and then cut with the long sword. You must examine this well and practice hitting.

Cut and Slash

To cut and slash are two different things. Cutting is decisive, with a resolute spirit. When you cut, your spirit is resolved. Slashing is nothing more than touching the enemy. Even if you slash strongly, and even if the enemy dies instantly, it is called slashing. If you first slash the enemy's hands or legs, you must then cut strongly. Slashing is in spirit the same as touching. When you understand this, they become indistinguishable. Learn this well.

Chinese Monkey's Body

The Chinese Monkey's Body is the spirit of not stretching out your arms. The spirit is to get in quickly with your whole body before the enemy attacks, without extending your arms in the least. When you come to within arm's reach it becomes easy to move your body in.

Glue and Lacquer Emulsion Body

The spirit of "Glue and Lacquer Emulsion Body" is to stick to the enemy and not separate from him. People tend to advance their head and legs quickly, but their body lags behind. Instead, when you approach the enemy, stick firmly with your head, body and legs. You should stick firmly so that there is not the slightest gap between the enemy's body and your body.

To Strive for Height

When you close with the enemy, strive with him for superior height without cringing. Stretch your legs, stretch your hips, and stretch your neck face to face with him. When you think you have won, and you are the higher, thrust in strongly. You must learn to execute this.

To Apply Stickiness

When both you and the enemy attack with the long sword, you should go in with a sticky feeling and fix your long sword against the enemy's as you receive his cut. The spirit of stickiness is not hitting very strongly, but hitting so that the long swords do not separate easily. It is best to approach as calmly as possible when hitting the enemy's long sword with stickiness. The difference between "Stickiness" and "Entanglement" is that stickiness is firm and entanglement is weak. It is important to understand this.

The Body Strike

The Body Strike means to approach the enemy through a gap in his guard. The spirit is to strike him with your body. Turn your face slightly aside and strike the enemy's breast with your left shoulder thrust out. Approach with a spirit of bouncing the enemy away, striking as strongly as possible in time with your breathing. If you succeed in this method of closing with the enemy, you will be able to knock him ten or twenty feet away. It is possible to strike the enemy until he is dead. Train vigorously.

Three Ways to Parry His Attack

There are three methods to parry a cut:

1) When the enemy makes an attack, dash his long sword to your right, as if thrusting at his eyes.
2) Parry by thrusting the enemy's long sword towards his right eye with the feeling of snipping his neck.
3) When you have a short "long sword", without worrying about parrying the enemy's long sword, close with him quickly by thrusting at his face with your left hand.

These are the three ways of parrying. You must bear in mind that you can always clench your left hand and thrust at the enemy's face with your fist. For this it is necessary to train well.

To Stab at the Face

When your spirit is intent on stabbing at the enemy's face, follow the line of the blades with the point of your long sword. If you are intent on stabbing at his face, his body will become disposable, presenting opportunities to win quickly. You must pursue the value of this technique through training.

To Stab at the Heart

The spirit of this principle is often useful when we become tired or for some reason our long sword will not cut. In fighting, if there are obstructions above or to the sides, and whenever it is difficult to cut, stabbing at the heart means to thrust at the enemy. You must stab the enemy's breast without letting the point of your long sword waver, showing the enemy the ridge of the blade square-on, and with the spirit of deflecting his long sword. You must be familiar with the application of this method.

To Scold "Tut-TUT!"

To "scold" means that when the enemy tries to counter-cut as you attack, you counter-cut again from below as if thrusting at him, trying to hold him down. With very quick timing you cut, scolding the enemy. Thrust up, "Tut!" and cut "TUT!" This timing is encountered time and time again in exchanges of blows. The way to scold "Tut-TUT" is to time the cut simultaneously with raising your long sword as if to thrust the enemy. This skill is acquired through repetitive practice.

The Smacking Parry

When you clash swords with the enemy, meet his attacking cut on your long sword with a *tee-dum, tee-dum* rhythm, smacking his sword and cutting him. The spirit of the smacking parry is not parrying, or smacking strongly, but smacking the enemy's long sword in accordance with his attacking cut, primarily intent on quickly cutting him. If you understand the timing of smacking, however hard your long swords clash, your sword point will not be knocked back even a little. You must study and train keenly in order to achieve this.

There are Many Enemies

"There are Many Enemies" applies when you are one fighting against many. Draw both sword and companion sword and assume a wide-stretched left and right attitude. The spirit is to chase the enemies from side to side, even though they come from all four directions. Observe their attacking order, and go to meet first those who attack first. Sweep your eyes around broadly, carefully examining the attacking order, and cut left and right alternately with your swords. Do not wait! Always quickly re-assume your attitudes to both sides, cutting the enemies down as they advance and crushing them in the direction from which they attack. Most importantly, aim to drive the enemy together, as if tying a line of fishes, and when they piled close together, cut them down strongly without giving them room to move.

One Cut

You can win with certainty with the spirit of "one cut", however it is difficult to attain this if you do not learn strategy well. If you train well in the Way, strategy will come from your heart and you will be able to win at will. You must train devotedly.

Direct Communication

The spirit of "Direct Communication" is how the true Way of the NiTo Ichi School is received and handed down. Strategy with the long sword cannot be clearly explained in writing, but through diligent practice you will understand how to win.

Oral tradition: "The true Way of strategy is revealed in the long sword."
Oral tradition: "Teach your body strategy."

Recorded in the above book is an outline of Ichi School sword fighting.
In summary, to learn how to win with the long sword in strategy, first learn the five approaches and the five attitudes, and absorb the Way of the long sword naturally in your body. You must understand spirit and timing, handle the long sword naturally, and move body and legs in harmony with your spirit. Whether beating one man or more, you will then appreciate the value of strategy.

Study the contents of this book taking one item at a time, and through fighting with enemies you will gradually come to know the principle of the Way.
Deliberately, with a patient spirit, absorb the virtue of the Way, occasionally raising your hand in combat. Maintain this spirit whenever you cross swords with an enemy.

Step by step walk the thousand-mile road.

Study strategy over the years and achieve the spirit of the warrior. Today is your victory over yourself of yesterday; tomorrow is your victory over lesser men.

In order to beat more skillful men, train intensely with the guidance of this book. Even if you kill an enemy, if it is not based on what you have learned it is not the true Way.

If you attain this Way of victory, you will be able to beat several tens of men. What remains is sword-fighting ability, which you can attain in battles and duels.

The Second Year of Shoho, the twelfth day of the fifth month (1645).

The Fire Book

I describe fighting as fire in this Fire Book of the NiTo Ichi School of strategy.

My Way of strategy is the sure method wherein "one man can beat ten; a thousand men can beat ten thousand". Of course, you cannot assemble a thousand or ten thousand men for everyday training. But you can become a master of strategy by training alone with a sword so that you can understand the enemy's strategies, his strengths and resources, and come to appreciate how to apply strategy to beat ten thousand enemies to win.

Most people think narrowly about the benefit of strategy. By using only their fingertips, they only know the benefit of three of the five inches of the wrist. They let a contest be decided merely by the span of their forearms, for they specialize in the small matter of dexterity, learning such trifles as hand and leg movements with the bamboo practice sword.

In my strategy, the training for killing enemies is by way of many contests, fighting for survival, discovering the meaning of life and death, learning the Way of the sword, judging the strength of attacks and understanding the Way of the "edge and ridge" of the sword. You cannot profit from small techniques particularly when full armor is worn.

Any man who wants to master the essence of my strategy must study diligently, training morning and evening. Thus can he polish his skill, become free from self, and realize extraordinary ability. He will come to possess miraculous power.

This is the practical result of strategy.

Depending on the Place

Examine your environment.

Take up an attitude with the sun behind you. If the situation does not allow this, you must try to keep the sun on your right side; or, if in buildings, stand with the entrance behind you or to your right. Make sure that your rear is unobstructed, and that there is free space on your left, your right side being occupied with your sword attitude. At night, if the enemy can be seen, keep the fire behind you and the entrance to your right, and otherwise take up your attitude as above. You must look down on the enemy, and take up your attitude on a slightly higher plane.

During a fight, always endeavor to chase the enemy around to your left side. Chase him towards awkward places - bad footholds, obstacles at the side, and so on - trying to keep him with his back to awkward places. When the enemy gets into an inconvenient position, do not let him look around, but conscientiously chase him around and pin him down. In houses, chase the enemy into the thresholds, lintels, doors, verandas, pillars, and so on, again not letting him see his situation. Use the virtues of each place to establish predominant positions from which to fight. You must research and train diligently in this.

The Three Methods to Forestall the Enemy

The first method is to forestall him by attacking. This is called *Ken No Sen* (to set him up).
Another method is to forestall him as he attacks. This is called *Tai No Sen* (to wait for the initiative).
The third method is when you and the enemy attack together. This is called *Tai Tai No Sen* (to accompany him and forestall him).
There are no methods of taking the lead other than these three. Since you can win quickly by taking the lead, this is one of the most important elements in strategy. There are several things involved in taking the lead. You must make the best of the situation, see through the enemy's spirit so that you grasp his strategy, and defeat him. It is impossible to fully explain this in writing.

The First - Ken No Sen

When you decide to attack, stay calm and dash in quickly, forestalling the enemy. Or, you can advance seemingly strongly but with a reserved spirit, forestalling him with the reserve.

Alternately, advance with as strong a spirit as possible, and when you reach the enemy move with your feet a little quicker than normal, unsettling him and overwhelming him sharply.

Or, with your spirit calm, attack with a feeling of constantly crushing the enemy, from first to last. The spirit is to win in the depths of the enemy.

These are all *Ken No Sen.*

The Second - Tai No Sen

When the enemy attacks, remain undisturbed but feign weakness. As the enemy approaches you, move away suddenly as if indicating that you intend to jump aside; then dash in attacking strongly as soon as you see the enemy relax. This is one way.
Or, as the enemy attacks, attack more strongly, taking advantage of the resulting disorder in his timing to win.

This is the *Tai No Sen* principle.

The Third - Tai Tai No Sen

When the enemy makes a quick attack, you must attack strongly and calmly, aim for his weak point as he draws near, and strongly defeat him.

Or, if the enemy attacks calmly, you must observe his movement and, with your body rather floating, join in with his movements as he draws near. Move quickly and cut him strongly.

This is *Tai Tai No Sen*

These things cannot be clearly explained in words. In these three ways of forestalling, you must judge each situation independently. In strategy, you have effectively won when you forestall the enemy, so you must study what is written here and train well to attain this.

To Hold Down a Pillow

In contests of strategy, you always want to lead the enemy about rather than be led about by the enemy. Obviously, the enemy will be endeavoring to do the same thing, but he cannot forestall you if you do not allow him to come out.

In strategy, you must stop the enemy as he attempts to cut; you must push down his thrust, and throw off his hold when he tries to grapple. This is the meaning of "to hold down a pillow"; it means not allowing the enemy's head to rise. When you have grasped this principle, you will see in advance whatever the enemy tries to bring about in the fight and suppress it. The spirit is to check his attack as soon as it begins.

The important thing in strategy is to suppress the enemy's useful actions but allow his useless actions. However, doing this alone is defensive. First, you must act according to the Way, suppress the enemy's techniques, foiling his plans, and thence command him directly. When you can do this you will be a master of strategy. You must train well and research "holding down a pillow".

Crossing at a Ford

"Crossing at a ford" means, for example, crossing the sea at a strait, knowing the route, knowing the soundness of your ship and the favor of the day. It means setting sail when conditions are good, and there is perhaps a favorable wind, or a tailwind. This spirit, if you attain it, applies to everyday life. You must always think of crossing at a ford.

In strategy also it is important to "cross at a ford". Discern the enemy's capability and, knowing your own strong points, "cross the ford" at the most advantageous place, as a good captain crosses a sea route. If you succeed in crossing at the best place, you may take your ease. To cross at a ford means to attack the enemy's weak point and to put yourself in an advantageous position. This is how to win in large-scale strategy. The spirit of crossing at a ford is necessary in both large- and small-scale strategy. You must examine this well.

To Know the Times

"To know the times" means to know the enemy's disposition in battle. Is it flourishing or waning? By observing the spirit of the enemy's men, you can discover the enemy's disposition and move your men into position accordingly, thereby fighting from a position of advantage.

In a duel, forestall the enemy and attack when you have recognized his school of strategy, perceived his quality, and his strong and weak points. If your ability to "know the times" is high, you will be able to attack in an unsuspecting manner, knowing his metre and modulation and the appropriate timing.

When you are thoroughly conversant with strategy, you will recognize the enemy's intentions and thus have many opportunities to win. You must sufficiently study this.

To Tread Down the Sword

"To tread down the sword" is a principle often used in strategy. In large-scale strategy, when the enemy first attacks by discharging bows and guns, it is difficult to attack if we are busy loading powder into our guns or notching our arrows. The spirit is to attack quickly while the enemy is still shooting with bows or guns. The spirit is to win by "treading down" as we receive the enemy's attack.

In single combat, we cannot get a decisive victory by cutting, with a "tee-dum tee-dum" feeling, in the wake of the enemy's attacking long sword. We must defeat him at the start of his attack, in the spirit of treading him down with the feet, so that he cannot rise again to the attack.

"Treading" does not simply mean treading with the feet. Tread with the body, tread with the spirit, and, of course, tread and cut with the long sword. You must achieve the spirit of not allowing the enemy to attack a second time. This is the spirit of forestalling in every sense. Once at the enemy, you should not aspire to merely strike him, but to cling after the attack. You must absorb this deeply.

To Know "Collapse"

Everything can collapse. Houses, bodies, and enemies all collapse when their rhythm becomes deranged. In large-scale strategy, when the enemy starts to collapse, you must pursue him without letting the opportunity pass by. If you fail to take advantage of your enemies' collapse, they may recover.

In single combat, the enemy sometimes loses timing and collapses. If you let this chance go by, he may recover and not be so negligent thereafter. Fix your eye on the enemy's collapse and chase him, attacking so that you do not let him recover. You must do this. The chasing attack is with a strong spirit. You must utterly cut the enemy down so that he does not recover his position. You must understand utterly how to cut down the enemy.

To Become the Enemy

"To become the enemy" means to think yourself into the enemy's position. In large-scale strategy, people are always under the impression that the enemy is strong, and so tend to become cautious. But if you have good soldiers, and if you understand the principles of strategy, and if you know how to beat the enemy, there is nothing to worry about.

In single combat also you must put yourself in the enemy's position. If you think, "Here is a master of the Way, who knows the principles of strategy" then you will surely lose. You must consider this deeply.

To Release Four Hands

"To Release Four Hands" is used when you and the enemy are contending with the same spirit, and the issue cannot be decided. Abandon this spirit and win through an alternative resource.

In large-scale strategy, when there is a "four hands" spirit, immediately throw away the current spirit and win with a technique the enemy does not expect.

Similarly, in single combat, when we think we have fallen into the "four hands" situation, we must defeat the enemy by changing our mind and applying a suitable technique according to his condition. You must be able to judge this.

To Move the Shade

"To move the shade" is used when you cannot see the enemy's spirit. In large-scale strategy, if you cannot see the enemy's position, indicate that you are about to attack strongly, so as to discover his resources. Once you observe his resources, it is then easy to defeat him with a different method.

In single combat, if the enemy takes up a rear or side attitude of the long sword so that you cannot see his intention, make a feint attack, and the enemy will show his long sword, thinking he sees your spirit. Benefiting from what you are shown, you can win with certainty. If you are negligent you will miss the timing. Research this well.

To Hold Down a Shadow

"Holding down a shadow" is used when you can see the enemy's attacking spirit. In large-scale strategy, when the enemy embarks on an attack, if you make a show of strongly suppressing his technique, he will change his mind. Then, altering your spirit, defeat him by forestalling him with a Void spirit.

Or, in single combat, hold down the enemy's strong intention with a suitable timing, and defeat him by forestalling him with this timing. Look well into this.

To Pass On

In large-scale strategy, when the enemy is agitated and shows an inclination to rush, do not be bothered in the least. Make a show of complete calmness, and the enemy will be taken in by this and will also relax. When you see that your spirit has been passed on, you can bring about the enemy's defeat by attacking strongly with a Void spirit.

In single combat, you can win by relaxing your body and spirit and then, taking advantage of the moment the enemy relaxes, attack strongly and quickly, forestalling him.

What is known as "getting someone drunk" is similar to this. You can also infect the enemy with a bored, careless, or weak spirit. Understand this and use it well.

To Cause Loss of Balance

Many things can cause a loss of balance - danger, hardship, and the element of surprise. In large-scale strategy it is important to cause loss of balance. Attack without warning where the enemy is not expecting it, and while his spirit is undecided, follow up your lead advantage and defeat him.

Or, in single combat, start by making a show of being slow, then suddenly attack strongly. Without allowing him time to breathe and to recover from the fluctuation of spirit, grasp the opportunity to win. Get the feel of this.

To Frighten

Fright often occurs, caused by the unexpected. In large-scale strategy you can frighten the enemy by shouting, making a small force seem large, or by threatening them from the flank without warning. These things all frighten. You can win by making best use of the enemy's frightened rhythm.

In single combat also, you must use the advantage of taking the enemy unawares by frightening him with your body, long sword, or voice to defeat him.

To Soak In

When you are struggling together with the enemy and you realize that you cannot advance, you should "soak in" and become one with the enemy. You can win by applying a suitable technique while you are mutually entangled.

In battles involving large numbers as well as in fights with small numbers, you can often win decisively with the advantage of knowing how to "soak" into the enemy, whereas, were you to draw apart, you would lose the chance to win. Study this well.

To Injure the Corners

It is difficult to move strong things by pushing directly, so you should "injure the corners". In large-scale strategy, it is beneficial to strike at the corners of the enemy's force, for if the corners are overthrown, the spirit of the whole body will be overthrown. To defeat the enemy you must follow up the attack when the corners have fallen.

In single combat, when you injure the "corners" of the enemy's body and weaken him, it is easy to collapse the enemy and to win. It is important to know how to do this, so you must practice keenly.

To Throw into Confusion

In large-scale strategy, our troops can confuse the enemy on the field. Observing the enemy's spirit, we can make him think, "Here? There? Like that? Like this? Slow? Fast?" Victory is certain when the enemy is caught up in a rhythm that confuses his spirit.

In single combat, we can confuse the enemy by attacking with varied techniques when the chance arises. Feint a thrust or cut, or make the enemy thing you are going close to him, and when he is confused you can easily win.

This is the essence of fighting, and you must research it deeply.

The Three Shouts

The voice is a thing of life. The voice shows energy. The three shouts are divided thus: before, during and after. Shout according to the situation.

In large-scale strategy, at the start of battle we shout as loudly as possible. During the fight, the voice is low-pitched, shouting out as we attack. After the contest, we shout in the wake of our victory. These are the three shouts.

In single combat, we make as if to cut and shout "Ei!" at the same time to disturb the enemy, then in the wake of our shout we cut with the long sword. We shout after we have cut down the enemy to announce victory. This is called "*sen go no koe*" (before and after voice). We do not shout simultaneously with flourishing the long sword. We shout during the fight to get into rhythm. Study this intensely.

To Mingle

'Mingling' is the spirit of advancing and becoming engaged with the enemy without retreating even one step. In battles, attack the enemy's strong points and when you see that they are beaten back, quickly separate and attack yet another strong point on the periphery of his force. The spirit of this is like a winding mountain path.

This is an important fighting method for one man against many. Strike down the enemies in one quarter, or drive them back, then grasp the timing and attack further strong points to right and left, as if on a winding mountain path, weighing the enemies' disposition. When you know the enemies' level, attack strongly with no trace of retreating spirit.

In single combat, too, use this spirit with the enemy's strong points.

To Crush

In large-scale strategy, when we see that the enemy has few men, or that he has many men but his spirit is weak and disordered, we knock the hat over his eyes, crushing him utterly. If we crush lightly, he may recover. You must learn the spirit of crushing as if with a hand-grip.

In single combat, if the enemy is less skillful, his rhythm disorganized, or if he has fallen into evasive or retreating attitudes, we must crush him immediately, without allowing him space to breathe. It is essential to crush him all at once. The essential thing is not to let him recover his position in the slightest.

The Mountain-Sea Change

The "mountain-sea" spirit means that it is poor strategy to repeat the same technique several times when fighting the enemy. If you must do something twice, do not try it a third time; for if you attack once and fail, there is little chance of succeeding if you use the same approach again. You must change your attacking method.

If the enemy thinks mountains, attack like the sea; and if he thinks of the sea, attack like mountains. You must research this deeply.

To Penetrate the Depths

The principle of "penetrating the depths" is to destroy the enemy's spirit. When we are fighting the enemy, even when it appears that we can win with the benefit of the Way, if his spirit is not extinguished he may be beaten superficially yet remain undefeated in spirit deep inside. Hence, we destroy the enemy's spirit in its depths, demoralizing him by quickly changing our spirit.

Penetrating the depths means penetrating with the long sword, penetrating with the body, and penetrating with the spirit. Once we have crushed the enemy in the depths, there is no need to remain spirited. But otherwise we must remain spirited. If the enemy remains spirited it is difficult to crush him. You must train in penetrating the depths for both large-scale and single combat strategy.

To Renew

"To renew" applies when we are fighting with the enemy and an entangled spirit arises where there is no possible resolution. In such a case we must abandon our efforts, think of the situation in a fresh spirit, and then win in the new rhythm. To renew when we are deadlocked with the enemy means that without changing our circumstance we change our spirit and win through a different technique.

It is necessary to consider how "to renew" also applies in large-scale strategy. Research this diligently.

Rat's Head, Ox's Neck

"Rat's head and ox's neck" means that, when we are fighting with the enemy and both he and we have become occupied with small points in an entangled spirit, we must always think of the Way of strategy as being both a rat's head and an ox's neck. Whenever we have become preoccupied with small details, we must suddenly change into a large spirit, interchanging large with small.

This is one of the essences of strategy. It is necessary that the warrior think in this spirit in everyday life. You must not depart from this spirit in large-scale strategy nor in single combat.

The Commander Knows the Troops

Using the wisdom of strategy, think of the enemy as your own troops. When you think in this way, you will be able to move the enemy at will and chase him around. Thus you become the general and the enemy becomes your troops. "The commander knows the troops" applies everywhere in fights in my Way of strategy. Master this.

To Let Go the Hilt

There are various kinds of spirit involved in letting go the hilt. There is the spirit of winning without a sword. There is also the spirit of holding the long sword but not winning. The various methods cannot be expressed in writing. You must train well.

The Body of a Rock

When you have mastered the Way of strategy, you can suddenly make your body like a rock, and then ten thousand things cannot touch or move you. This is the body of a rock.

All that is recorded above are my thoughts about Ichi School sword fencing, written down as the thoughts came to me. This is the first time I have written about my technique, and the order of things is a bit confused. It is difficult to express these concepts clearly.

This book is intended as a spiritual guide for the man who wishes to learn the Way. My heart has been inclined to the Way of strategy from my youth onwards. I have devoted myself to training my hand, tempering my body, and attaining the many spiritual attitudes of sword fencing.

If one observes men of other schools discussing theory and concentrating on techniques with the hands, although they seem skillful to watch, they have not the slightest true spirit. Of course, they think they are training the body and spirit, but it is an obstacle to the true Way, and its negative influence remains forever. Thus the true Way of strategy is degenerating and dying out.

The true Way of sword fencing entails the craft of defeating the enemy in a fight, and nothing other than this. If you attain and adhere to the wisdom of my strategy, you need never doubt that you will win.

The second year of Shoho, the fifth month, the twelfth day (1645).

The Wind Book

In strategy, you must be familiar with the Ways of other schools, so I have written about various other traditions of strategy in this Wind Book.

Without knowledge of the Ways of other schools, it is difficult to understand the essence of my Ichi School. Looking at other schools, we find some that specialize in techniques of strength using extra-long swords; some study the Way of the short sword, known as *kodachi;* some teach dexterity in large numbers of sword techniques, teaching attitudes of the sword as the "surface" and the Way as the "interior".

However, in this book, in which I point out all the vices and virtues, and rights and wrongs, I will show that none of these are the true Way. My Ichi School is different. Other schools make success their means of livelihood, decoratively coloring articles in order to sell them. This is definitely not the Way of strategy.

Many of the world's strategists are concerned only with sword fencing, and limit their training to flourishing the long sword and carriage of the body. But is dexterity alone sufficient to win? This is not the essence of the Way.

I have recorded the unsatisfactory points of other schools one by one in this book. You must study these matters deeply to appreciate the benefit of my NiTo Ichi School.

Other Schools Using Extra-Long Swords

Some other schools have a liking for extra-long swords. From the point of view of my strategy these must be seen as weak schools, for they do not appreciate the principle of cutting the enemy by any means. Their preference is for the extra-long sword and, relying on the virtue of its length, they think of defeating the enemy from a distance.

In this world it is said, "One inch gives the hand advantage", but these are the idle words of one who does not know strategy. It shows the inferior strategy of a weak sprit that men should depend on the length of their sword, fighting from a distance without the benefit of strategy.

I expect there is a case for liking extra-long swords as part of a school's doctrine, but if we compare this with real life it is unreasonable. Surely we need not necessarily be defeated if we are using a short sword, and have no long sword?
It is difficult for these people to cut the enemy when at close quarters because of the length of the long sword. The large blade path makes the long sword an encumbrance, and they are at a disadvantage compared to the man armed with a short companion sword.

There is an old saying: "Great and small go together." I do not unconditionally dislike extra-long swords; what I dislike is the inclination towards the long sword. If we consider large-scale strategy, we can think of large forces in terms of long swords, and small forces as short swords. Cannot few men give battle against many? There are many instances of few men overcoming many.

If your heart is inclined to the long sword, your strategy is useless when called on to fight in a confined space, or if you are in a house armed only with your companion sword. Besides, some men have not the strength of others.

In my doctrine, I dislike preconceived, narrow spirit. You must study this well.

The Strong Long Sword Spirit in Other Schools

You should not speak of strong and weak long swords. If you are concerned with the strength of your sword, you will try to cut unreasonably strongly, and will not be able to cut at all. It is equally bad to try to cut strongly when testing the sword.

Whenever you cross swords with an enemy you must not think of cutting him either strongly or weakly; think only of cutting and killing him. Be intent solely on killing the enemy.

If you rely on strength, when you hit the enemy's sword you will inevitably hit too hard. If you do this, your own sword will be carried along as a result. Thus the saying, "The strongest hand wins", has no meaning.

In large-scale strategy, if you have a strong army and are relying on strength to win, but the enemy also has a strong army, the battle will be fierce. This is the same for both sides. Without the correct principle the fight cannot be won.

The spirit of my school is to win through the wisdom of strategy, paying no attention to trifles. Learn this well.

Use of the Shorter Long Sword in Other Schools

Using a shorter long sword is not the true Way to win.

In ancient times, *tachi* and *katana* meant long and short swords. Men of superior strength in the world can wield even a long sword lightly, so there is no case for their liking the short sword. They also make use of the length of spears and halberds. Some men use a shorter long sword with the intention of jumping in and stabbing the enemy at the unguarded moment when he flourishes his sword. This inclination is not the true Way.

To aim for the enemy's unguarded moment is completely defensive, and undesirable at close quarters with the enemy. Furthermore, you cannot use the method of jumping inside his defense with a short sword if there are many enemies. Some men think that if they go against many enemies with a shorter long sword they can unrestrictedly frisk around cutting in sweeps, but they have to parry cuts continuously, and eventually become entangled with the enemy. This is inconsistent with the true Way of strategy.

The sure Way to win is rather to chase the enemy around in a confusing manner, causing him to jump aside, with your body held strongly and straight. The same principle applies to large-scale strategy. The essence of strategy is to fall upon the enemy in large numbers and to bring about his speedy downfall.

Through their study of strategy, people of the world became accustomed to countering, evading and retreating as the normal thing. Becoming set in this habit, they are easily paraded around by the enemy. The Way of strategy is straight and true. You must chase the enemy around and make him obey your spirit.

Other Schools with many Methods of using the Long Sword

In order to gain the admiration of beginners, other schools teach that there are many methods of using the long sword. This is selling the Way. It is a vile spirit in strategy.

The reason for this is that to deliberate over many ways of cutting down a man is an error. To begin with, killing is not the Way of mankind. Killing is the same for people who are experienced fighters and for those who are not. It is the same for women or children, and there are not many different methods. We can speak of different tactics such as stabbing and mowing down, but only of these.

Anyway, cutting down the enemy is the Way of strategy, and there is no need for many refinements of it.

Even so, according to the place, your long sword may be obstructed above or to the sides, so you will need to hold your sword in such a manner that it can be used. There are five methods to win, in five directions. Methods apart from these five - hand twisting, body bending, jumping out, and so on, to cut the enemy - are not the true Way of strategy. In order to cut the enemy you must not make twisting or bending cuts. These are completely useless.

In my strategy, I bear my spirit and body straight, and cause the enemy to twist and bend. The necessary spirit is to win by attacking the enemy when his spirit is warped. You must understand this well.

Use of Attitudes of the Long Sword in Other Schools

Placing a great deal of importance on the attitudes of the long sword is a mistaken way of thinking. Attitudes are defensive techniques for situations in which you are not to be moved. That is, for garrisoning castles, battle array, and so on, showing the spirit of not being moved even by a strong assault. I dislike the defensive spirit known as "attitude".

In the Way of dueling, however, you must always be intent upon taking the lead and attacking. Attitude is the spirit of awaiting an attack. You must appreciate this.
In duels of strategy you must move the opponent's attitude: Attack where his spirit is lax, throw him into confusion,

irritate and terrify him. Take advantage of the enemy's rhythm when he is unsettled and you can win.

I dislike the defensive spirit known as "attitude", therefore in my Way, there is something called "Attitude-No Attitude".

In large-scale strategy we deploy our troops for battle bearing in mind our strength, observing the enemy's numbers, and noting the details of the battlefield. This is at the start of the battle.

The spirit of attacking is completely different from the spirit of being attacked. Bearing an attack well, with a strong attitude, and parrying the enemy's attack well, is like making a wall of spears and halberds. When you attack the enemy, your spirit must go to the extent of pulling the stakes out of a wall and using them as spears and halberds. You must examine this well.

Fixing the Eyes in Other Schools

Some schools maintain that the eyes should be fixed on the enemy's long sword; some fix the eye on the hands, some on the face, some on the feet, and so on. If you fix the eyes on these places your spirit can become confused, and your strategy thwarted.

I will explain this in detail. Football players do not fix their eyes on the ball, but by knowing how to play well they perform well. When you become accustomed to something, you are not limited to the use of your eyes. People such as master musicians have the music score in front of their nose, but this does not mean that they fix their eyes on it specifically. Similarly, fighters flourish the sword in several ways when they have mastered the Way, but this does not mean that they make pointless movements of the sword. It means that they can perform naturally.

In the Way of strategy, once you have fought many times you will easily be able to appraise the speed and position of the enemy's sword, and having mastery of the Way you will see the weight of his spirit. In strategy, fixing the eyes means gazing at the man's heart.

In large-scale strategy the area to observe is the enemy's strength. "Perception" and "sight" are the two methods of seeing. Perception consists of concentrating strongly on the enemy's spirit, observing the condition of the battle field, fixing the gaze strongly, seeing the progress of the fight and the changes of advantage. This is the sure way to win.

In single combat you must not fix the eyes on details. As I said before, if you fix your eyes on details and neglect important things, your spirit will become bewildered, and victory will escape you. Research this principle well and train diligently.

Use of the Feet in Other Schools

There are various methods of using the feet: floating foot, jumping foot, springing foot, treading foot, crow's foot, and such nimble walking methods. From the point of view of my strategy, these are all unsatisfactory.

I dislike floating foot because the feet always tend to float during the fight. The Way must be trod firmly. Neither do I like jumping foot, because it encourages the habit of jumping, and a jumpy spirit. However much you jump, there is no real justification for it. Springing foot causes a springing spirit which is indecisive. Treading foot is a "waiting" method which I especially dislike.

Apart from these, there are various fast walking methods, such as crow's foot, and so on. However, sometimes you may encounter the enemy on marshland, swampy ground, river valleys, stony ground, or narrow roads, situations in which you cannot jump or move the feet quickly.

In my strategy, the footwork does not change. I always walk as I usually do in the street. You must never lose control of your feet. Move fast or slowly according to the enemy's rhythm, adjusting your body only as needed.

Carrying the feet is also important in large-scale strategy, for if you attack quickly and thoughtlessly without knowing the enemy's spirit, your rhythm will become deranged and you will not be able to win. Or, if you advance too slowly, you will not be able to take advantage of the enemy's disorder, the opportunity to win will escape, and you will not be able to finish the fight quickly. You must win by seizing upon the enemy's disorder and derangement, and by not according him even the slightest hope of recovery. Practice this well.

Speed in Other Schools

Speed is not part of the true Way of strategy. Whatever the Way, the master of strategy does not appear fast.

Some people can walk as fast as a hundred or a hundred and twenty miles in a day, but this does not mean that they run continuously from morning till night. Unpracticed runners may seem to have been running all day, but their performance is poor.

In the Way of dance, accomplished performers can sing while dancing, but when beginners try this they slow down and their spirit becomes busy. Very skillful people can manage a fast rhythm, but if you try to beat too quickly you will get out of time. Of course, slowness is also bad. Truly skilled people never get out of rhythm, are always deliberate, and never appear busy. From this example, the principle can be seen.

Speed is especially counterproductive in the Way of strategy. The reason for this is that depending on the place - marsh or swamp and so on - it may not be possible to move the body and legs together quickly. If you have a long sword in this situation you will be able to cut quickly even less, and if you try to cut quickly, as if using a fan or short sword, you will actually not cut at all. You must appreciate this.

In large-scale strategy, a fast, busy spirit is also undesirable. The spirit must be that of holding down a pillow, for then you will not be even a little off time.

When your opponent is hurrying recklessly, you must act contrarily and stay calm, without being influenced by the opponent. Train diligently to attain this spirit.

"Interior" and "Surface" in Other Schools

The artistic accomplishments usually claim surface meaning, and inner meaning (secret tradition) or "interior" and "gate", but in my Way of strategy, there is no "interior", nor "surface".

In combat there is no such thing as fighting on the surface, or cutting with the interior. When I teach my Way, I first train pupils in techniques that are easy for them to understand, and gradually endeavor to explain the deep principles, according to the pupil's progress. In any event, because the way to understanding is through experience, I do not speak of "interior" and "gate".

In this world, if you go into the mountains, and decide to go deeper and yet deeper, instead you will emerge at the gate. Whatever is the Way, it has an interior, and it is sometimes a good thing to point out the gate. In strategy, we cannot say what is concealed and what is revealed.

Perceiving the ability of my pupils, I teach the direct Way, remove the bad influence of other schools, and gradually introduce them to the true Way of the warrior. The method of teaching my strategy is with a trustworthy spirit.

In the above sections, I have tried to record an outline of the strategy of other schools. I could continue by giving a specific accounting of these schools one by one, from the "gate" to the "interior", but I have intentionally not named the schools or their main points. The reason for this is that different branches of schools give different interpretations of the doctrines. In as much as men's opinions differ, so there must be differing ideas on the same matter. Thus no one man's conception is valid for any school.

I have shown the general tendencies of other schools on nine points. If we look at them from an honest viewpoint, we see that people tend to like long swords or short swords, and become concerned with strength in both large and small matters. You can see why I do not deal with the "gates" of other schools.

In my Ichi School of the long sword there is neither gate nor interior. There is no inner meaning in sword attitudes. You must simply keep your spirit true to realize the virtue of strategy.

Twelfth day of the fifth month, the second year of Shoho (1645)

The Book of the Void

The spirit of the void is where there is nothing. By knowing things that exist, you can know that which does not exist. That is the void. It is not part of man's general knowledge.

People in this world look at things mistakenly, thinking that what they do not understand must be the void. This is not the true void. It is bewilderment. Similarly, in the Way of strategy, there are warriors who think that whatever they cannot understand in their craft is the void. This is not the true void.

To attain the Way of strategy as a warrior you must train completely in other martial arts and not deviate for a moment from Way of the warrior. Practice day in and day out with a settled spirited. Polish the twofold spirit heart and mind, and sharpen the twofold gaze perception and sight. When your spirit is no longer foggy, when the clouds of bewilderment clear away, there is the true void.

Until you realize the true Way, whether it be Buddhism or common sense, you may think that things are correct and in order. However, if we look at things objectively, from the viewpoint of laws of the world, we see various doctrines departing from the true Way. Know well this spirit, with forthrightness as the foundation and the true spirit as the Way. Enact strategy broadly, correctly and openly.

73

You will then come to think of things in a wide sense and, taking the void as the Way, you will see the Way as void.

The void consists only of virtue, and no evil. Wisdom exists, principle exists, the Way exists; spirit is nothingness.

Twelfth day of the fifth month, second year of Shoho (1645)

Lightning Source UK Ltd.
Milton Keynes UK
29 November 2010

163618UK00001B/39/A